RETHINKING
A MIDDLE EAST IN
TRANSITION

EDITED BY
KENNETH H. WILLIAMS

A joint publication of the Middle East Institute
and Marine Corps University Press

2011

This book documents the proceedings of the 64th Annual Conference of the Middle East Institute. The views expressed in it are solely those of the commentators. The Middle East Institute does not take positions on Middle East policy, and Marine Corps University Press is an entity of the U.S. government.

Middle East Institute
1761 N Street, NW
Washington, DC 20036-2882
www.mei.edu

Marine Corps University Press
3078 Upshur Avenue
Quantico, Virginia 22134
www.tecom.usmc.mil/mcu/mcupress

For sale by the Superintendent of Documents, U.S. Government Printing Office
Internet: bookstore.gpo.gov Phone: toll free (866) 512-1800; DC area (202) 512-1800
Fax: (202) 512-2104 Mail: Stop IDCC, Washington, DC 20402-0001

ISBN 978-0-16-090175-1

TABLE OF CONTENTS

KYRGYZSTAN

UZBEKISTAN

★ Tashkent

TURKMENISTAN

CHINA

TAJIKISTAN

★ Ashgabat

★ Dushanbe

bian

ea

★ Tehran

Kabul ★

IRAN

AFGHANISTAN

Islamabad ★

PAKISTAN

an

ulf

BAHRAIN

★ Manama

INDIA

★ QATAR

Doha

Abu

★ Dhabi

UNITED ARAB

EMIRATES

Muscat ★

N

OMAN

Arabian Sea

PREFACE

PREFACE

In his acceptance speech at the Middle East Institute's 64th Annual Conference, the recipient of the MEI Award for Excellence, former Deputy Prime Minister of Lebanon Issam M. Fares, said: "Let us hope that this year, a new spirit will move the region, from the cycle of inaction and despair to a current of forward development and just solutions. It does take spirit and resolve to break the cycle, and let us pray that your leaders and ours will have the necessary vision and courage to see this process through." Since Mr. Fares delivered these remarks, of course, that "new spirit" did move the region, and irrevocably so. The Jasmine Revolution blossomed in Tunisia and grew rapidly into the Arab Awakening that inspired revolution in Egypt and antigovernment protests in Bahrain, Yemen, Libya, and Syria. The historic events that shook the Middle East to its very core are reverberating still as this book goes to press, with unrest continuing to rock several Arab countries, while others prepare for their first free and fair elections ever.

When we conceived of "Rethinking a Middle East in Transition" as the theme for MEI's conference in November 2010, we did not know that these extraordinary events awaited the region just a few short months hence. And while we would like to take credit for our particularly timely conference title, our choice of theme was in reality less a matter of unusual foresight than a reflection of the state of the Middle East as we understood it at that time.

In the fall of 2010, the region stood at a critical juncture. Iran was growing in regional influence empowered by the fall of Saddam Hussein in 2003 and the increasing clout of Iranian-backed groups like Hezbollah and Hamas. Turkey's regional influence was also on the rise as a result of its good-neighbor policy and economic clout, while traditional regional power brokers Egypt and Saudi Arabia found themselves increasingly sidelined, in the shadow of their more activist neighbors. In addition, Israeli–Palestinian peace talks initiated that September had fizzled by the late fall, increasing popular Arab resentment not only toward Israel and the United States, but also toward Arab leaders for their perceived weakness.

Because so many of these issues were transnational in nature, affecting multiple countries in the region, we took a thematic rather than a geographic approach to the conference, aiming to explore a variety of issues as they manifested themselves throughout the Middle East. This tactic enabled us to approach key topics from multiple perspectives without boxing ourselves into the more limiting "one country, one panel" mode. For example, a panel entitled "U.S. Middle East Policy in the Second Half of the Obama Term" examined America's policy toward the region vis-à-vis security, the military, energy, and trade, rather than on a country-by-country basis. "Shifting Regional Dynamics: Turkey, Israel, Iran, and the Arab States" looked at the new power structure in the Middle East and the interplay of these actors on the regional stage. Recognizing that unofficial actors play an important role in the Middle East, our "New Approaches to Nonstate Armed Actors" panel explored the ways in which groups like Hamas and Hezbollah are shaping the agenda in the region, and how they can be either isolated or integrated into the state system in the countries in which they operate. Our last panel, "Reevaluating U.S. Policy in Afghanistan and Pakistan," anticipated the December 2010 policy review for U.S. strategy in Afghanistan and focused on America's relationship with those two countries and their relationship to each other. While this final panel was somewhat country-specific, our thinking for the conference overall was motivated by a desire to impart a holistic understanding of this complex region rather than merely a fragmented view of its many and diverse constituent parts.

On behalf of the Board of Governors, staff, scholars, and members of the Middle East Institute, it is with great pride that I introduce the publication of MEI's 64th Annual Conference transcripts. We at MEI hope that by publishing the contents of the conference, we will make the invaluable information shared at the event more widely accessible and available to the public, experts, and policy makers alike. The Annual Conference is a valuable tool for improving our collective understanding of the Middle East, the many and varied challenges it faces, and America's role in fostering security and development in the region for the future.

It is also my pleasure to launch MEI's collaboration with Marine Corps University Press, which is publishing this book. The Middle East Institute is especially grateful to the Marine Corps University Press for its interest in and support of our Institute and the work that we do.

Following the events of the early months of 2011, the entire world is now "rethinking" the Middle East during this period of unprecedented transition. The successes and failures of the Arab Spring remain to be seen, and the extent to which lasting change will take root is uncertain. Nevertheless, we hope the publication of *Rethinking a Middle East in Transition* will help readers better understand the regional conditions that preceded this historic period and provide them the background to better analyze what is now unfolding.

By continuing to host timely, relevant conferences and events that shed light on the regional changes playing out, the Middle East Institute will remain a leading voice in interpreting this complex region for policy makers and the interested public in Washington, across America, and around the world.

Wendy J. Chamberlin

President, Middle East Institute

June 2011

Women protest against the government in Tahrir Square in Cairo, Egypt, on February 8, 2011. The Mubarak government fell three days later.
(Corbis/EPA/Hannibal Hanschke)

INTRODUCTION

KENNETH H. WILLIAMS

I n the Middle East, change can take centuries to happen. Yet, as witnessed during the time that this book has been in preparation, it can also occur seemingly overnight. As U.S. President Barack H. Obama put it at the time that Egyptian President Hosni Mubarak stepped down in February 2011, "The wheel of history turned at a blinding pace."[1]

This book documents conditions and perceptions in the Middle East on the eve of the momentous events that began in the Muslim world in January 2011. The region was indeed "in transition"—more than the participants knew—when they convened in Washington, D.C., on November 3–4, 2010, for the Middle East Institute's 64th Annual Conference.[2] Indicative of the theme of the program, the underlying current for all of the panels was "where do we go from here?"—with the Middle East peace process; in dealing with Iran; in transitioning out of Iraq; in confronting nonstate actors; in examining the broader Middle East (including Turkey's emerging role); and in facing the ongoing conflict in Afghanistan and Pakistan.[3]

---

1 Office of the White House Press Secretary, "Remarks by the President on Egypt," White House, Washington, DC, February 11, 2011, http://www.whitehouse.gov/the-press-office/2011/02/11/remarks-president-egypt. For President Obama's major Middle East policy speech later in the "Arab Spring," see Office of the White House Press Secretary, "Remarks by the President on the Middle East and North Africa," Department of State, Washington, DC, May 19, 2011, http://www.whitehouse.gov/the-press-office/2011/05/19/remarks-president-middle-east-and-north-africa.

2 The November 3 portion of the conference was a banquet that featured an address by former President William J. Clinton. His remarks were off the record, so only the panel discussions from November 4 are presented in this book.

3 The Middle East Institute broadly defines the region about which it promotes study as an area stretching from Morocco to Pakistan to Central Asia.

Obama took office in 2009 promising progress in all of these areas. He immediately appointed special envoys for the Arab–Israeli peace process and for Afghanistan–Pakistan. His speech addressing the Muslim world in Cairo in June of that year was well received and widely praised.[4] According to conference panelist Shibley Telhami, polling in the Middle East in the spring of 2009 indicated that a plurality of Arabs had a favorable opinion of an American president, a first for the years that he and his group had been conducting their surveys. Polling in June and July 2010, however, found that Obama's approval rating in the Middle East had fallen below 20 percent. As Telhami put it, the expectations of the people of the region "were high—and they were raised by the Cairo speech, no doubt—and when, in their view, the administration didn't deliver, attitudes changed dramatically."

Obama's approval rating within the United States had declined as well, resulting in midterm elections (on November 2, right before the conference) that shifted control of the U.S. House of Representatives from the Democrats to the Republicans, presenting the president with a divided Congress. While foreign policy issues, specifically the Middle East concerns of the wars in Iraq and Afghanistan and engagement with Iran, were central to the 2008 campaign, the 2010 canvass focused on domestic issues, with little discussion of topics beyond America's borders. These remained pertinent, however, and interest in foreign affairs and Middle East issues remained high in Washington policy circles, resulting in a record number of attendees for the Middle East Institute's 2010 conference.

The first conference panel addressed several of the most pressing Middle East issues facing the administration: the Israeli–Palestinian peace process, Iraq, and Iran. David Makovsky called the time from when Obama took office at the beginning of 2009 through August 2010 a period of "opportunity utterly lost" in Arab–Israeli peace efforts. He pointed out that Obama inherited a very different political landscape than that of George W. Bush's second term, as Israeli Prime Minister Ehud Olmert had resigned and Israeli forces were fighting in Gaza until right before Obama's inauguration. The government that new Israeli Prime Minister Benjamin Netanyahu formed in 2009 took a harder line on the issues under negotiation. Palestinian National Authority President Mahmoud Abbas, whose elected term ended in January 2009, refused to cede power

---

4 Office of the White House Press Secretary, "Remarks by the President on a New Beginning," Cairo University, Cairo, Egypt, June 4, 2009, http://www.whitehouse.gov/the-press-office/remarks-president-cairo-university-6-04-09.

to Gaza-based Hamas. Abbas mistrusted Netanyahu and, as described by Makovsky, "felt trapped" by Obama's desire for a freeze on new Israeli settlements on the West Bank, a point that Abbas later came to insist upon himself. After describing further sticking points in the negotiations, Makovsky assessed the chances for progress in the near term and concluded that "even under the best of circumstances, it will be difficult for both peoples to solve all the differences."

Turning to Iraq, Joost R. Hiltermann reviewed the questionable decisions after the American-led Coalition invasion in 2003 that created what he termed three "vacuums"—political, security, and managerial. These voids beget conditions that resulted in "polarization and violence and, over time, sectarian war." He noted the military and psychological impact of the "surge" in 2008, which "showed Iraqis that the United States was still committed to Iraq" and led to relative stability by 2010.

With the impact of the surge "starting to peter out," Hiltermann was unsure of what would come next. He posited that Iraq is "at least a decade away" from truly benefitting from its wealth of natural resources. He advised that the United States not "smother" Iraq—"allow for a close partnership, but let it be a partnership," and "pay attention to Iraqi priorities."

The future remains unclear on how much the newly forming Iraqi government will be influenced by Iran and how open it and the Iraqi people will remain to partnership with the United States. Hiltermann suggested that if tensions escalate between the U.S. and Iran on the nuclear issue, "Iraq may become the battleground." He believed that the future of Iraq would very much depend on the state of U.S.–Iranian relations.

On that subject, Suzanne Maloney observed that while Obama had campaigned on making engagement with Iran a priority, the change in U.S. policy during the first two years of Obama's presidency was much more one of style than substance. Iran met the administration's initial engagement attempts with a "lack of reciprocity." In the wake of the tumultuous June 2009 Iranian presidential election and its aftermath, direct outreach by the United States became virtually impossible. With few other options, the Americans turned to employing more international pressure—including United Nations sanctions—to confront the increasing threat of Iran's nuclear program.[5]

---

5 United Nations Security Council Resolution 1929, adopted June 9, 2010, http://daccess-dds-ny.un.org/doc/UNDOC/GEN/N10/396/79/PDF/N1039679.pdf.

Maloney highlighted four "big political earthquakes" underway within Iran: the splintering of the conservatives; the elimination of the left wing; the "sidelining" of Akbar Hashemi Rafsanjani; and the rise of the Revolutionary Guard. Looking ahead, she believed that Iran would continue "dangling" the prospect of dialogue while being expected "to renege [on] or renegotiate" any potential agreement. Maloney discounted talk of a potential war between the United States and Iran and sketched what she saw as a more likely and also problematic scenario: an Iran that, because of the impact of sanctions, will grow "impoverished, more isolated, hollowed out, and more radicalized."

Edward P. Djerejian, in looking at the Middle East region as a whole, urged the Obama administration to move from conflict management to conflict resolution. Although America remains the "premier economic, military, and diplomatic power" in the world, Djerejian observed that the United States must recognize the limits of that power and not continue to overstretch itself by "constantly putting out fires" in the Middle East and other parts of the world. He pointed to the Arab–Israeli issue as the ongoing crux in the Arab world, as well as a recruitment impetus for Islamic radicalism. He placed resolution of the Palestinian question at the core of any broader Middle East solution and also advocated an Israeli–Lebanese settlement. During the question-and-answer period, Djerejian acknowledged European contributions to improving Israeli–Palestinian relations, but he concluded that "at the end of the day, it is really going to be the United States that has to be the major interlocutor between the Israelis and the Palestinians."

The second panel addressed various aspects of confronting nonstate actors—opposition groups and combatants that are not aligned with an existing country or government. Mitchell B. Reiss focused on the question of whether to negotiate with "terrorists," and if so, how? He offered four lessons from his research on engagement with insurgents, noting that the established state actor or group must demonstrate its resolve; it has to develop its intelligence resources; it needs to identify a viable leader or central group among the nonstate actors with whom to negotiate; and it must have patience. On the last point, Reiss emphasized that efforts at engagement may take years, possibly decades, citing in particular the British government's long-running and ultimately successful work with the Irish Republican Army. In the context of the Middle East, he examined American engagement with the sheikhs in al-Anbar Province in Iraq.

David Kilcullen discussed the challenges inherent when an international power intervenes in a fragile state, which may be home to multiple groups of violent nonstate actors. He advocated for "bottom-up, community-based peace building" rather than "top-down security operations" by international groups, with a focus on "enabling civil society to solve its own problems." He cited examples—some successful, some not—in Iraq, Afghanistan, and the Sudan. Kilcullen acknowledged the need for a military role in providing a relatively secure environment in which civil society can prosper but stated that it should be a "very limited, carefully targeted role." In responding to a question about Iraq and Afghanistan, he conceded that while he was part of the U.S. military's Iraq recalibration, "I'm not quite sure we know how we did it in Iraq. So I'm not sure we can pull it off again."

Robert Malley looked primarily at Hamas in Gaza and Hezbollah in Lebanon to address the question of what the objectives of the United States and other countries should be when dealing with nonstate actors. He argued that questions about whether the interested countries should talk with these groups have diverted attention from what should be the key point: whether the efforts of the international community have been successful. According to Malley, by nearly all measures, they have not. He opined that there should be more middle ground on the spectrum between direct negotiations and complete isolation. He also reiterated Reiss's point that many nonstate groups do not have leaders with the experience and control for them to be viable negotiating partners with the international powers.

Peter R. Neumann highlighted findings from his study of eight de-radicalization and disengagement programs, the majority of which are in the Middle East. Most are operated in prisons. He listed several attributes of programs generally thought to have been successful, including a diversity of approaches; credible trainers; and emphasis on transition of the de-radicalized back into society, guided by commitments and incentives. A major caveat, according to Neumann, is that de-radicalization programs "cannot really be studied in isolation of the conflicts in which they are being implemented," and without understanding the progression of those conflicts. As an example, he argued that the de-radicalization program in Iraq in 2007–8 that is generally described as successful would have produced different and likely less useful results in 2005. According to Neumann, the change in circumstances in the country and the conflict in the intervening years made a substantial difference.

The third panel looked at the shifting dynamics of the wider region. Ömer Taşpınar explored what he called Turkey's "new activist, engagement-oriented foreign policy," which he sees as a product of increasing democratization and concern by the government about public opinion. According to Taşpınar, the country is becoming more conservative, more nationalist, and more of an independent actor. He demurred from calling the shift "Islamization," preferring to say that Turkey is "coming to terms with its Muslim identity" and feeling more solidarity with the Arab world. That connection has been strengthened in tangible terms as well as ideological ones, as Turkish trade with the Middle East has quadrupled over the last decade.

Taşpınar observed that the Kurdish question had dominated Turkey's foreign policy since the end of the Cold War and also hurt its image in the Arab world. Within the last five years, however, as he described it, the Turks decided that it would be better to "co-opt" the Kurds than to confront them, to basically let it be known that Turkey would let the Kurds coexist as long as they are not harboring groups like the PKK.[6] The relative improvement of Turkish–Kurdish relations, in turn, has allowed for more Turkish interaction with the Middle East.

Like much of the Middle East, Turkey is struggling with the question of how to engage with Iran, and to what extent. Turkey's relations with Israel, meanwhile, have declined in recent years, a shift that Taşpınar sees as due primarily to increasing responsiveness to public opinion by the current government.

Alex Vatanka focused on Iran and its regional interaction. Instead of Iran "rising" in Middle Eastern prominence, as some have claimed, Vatanka sees its recent activity more as filling regional vacuums that have developed for various reasons, including the toppling of Iran's former counterweight, Saddam Hussein's Iraq. Iran is also "helping entities that are looking for sponsors," such as Hezbollah and Hamas. Vatanka emphasized that this need for support should not be taken as a shift of thinking on the part

---

6 Partiya Karkerên Kurdistan (PKK), the Kurdistan Workers' Party.

of Arab countries toward the Islamic Republic model. This opinion, however, seems to hold sway within the Iranian government, where there is also a belief that the neighboring regimes will fall, leaving Iran even larger voids to fill.

Vatanka also pointed to Iran's "contradictory policy" of trying to convince Arab states, especially those on the Persian Gulf, that they would benefit from driving Western influence—particularly that of the United States—out of the region. Such a policy would be contradictory for these countries because most depend on the United States for security (including protection from Iran), and all benefit immeasurably from Western oil dollars.

From the Israeli point of view, Itamar Rabinovich stated that Israel sees Iran as its number-one threat, not so much in the nuclear-weapons sense, but more broadly because of Iran's desire to be the "regional hegemon." He described Iran's nuclear ambitions more in terms of a defensive mechanism, as an "umbrella" that would give Iran more freedom to exert its influence in the region without fear of reprisal.

Rabinovich also noted Turkey's growing regional interests. He did not think that Turkey would be joining the Iranian camp (including Syria, Hezbollah, and Hamas) but in many ways felt that Turkey was reinforcing "the direction in which [Iran] is trying to take the region." Noting the mediation that Turkey provided between Israel and Syria in 2008–9, he stated that Turkey could still play a role in the peace process, but not if it chooses to support Hamas.

Shibley Telhami offered perspective on the region based on the surveys he supervised in six Arab states in mid–2010. He began with the statistic that roughly 90 percent of Arabs view Israel as the greatest threat to them personally, with the United States second on the list at around 80 percent. Iran was a far-distant third at only 10 percent. He stressed that the Arab public looks at the world "through the prism" of the Arab–Israeli issue. Telhami explained that many Arabs see Iran as the "enemy of my enemy"—Israel, and in some cases the United States—and that most favorable leanings toward Iran are more a reflection of this dynamic than of a desire that their countries emulate or partner with Iran. As for their governments, according to Telhami, "There is no question that Arab governments across the board worry about the rise of

Iranian influence," but the fear of the spread of influence is different from the threat of actual attack.

Telhami also observed that across the region, there is a sense that the "relative power of the Arab world has diminished." In the eyes of the Arab elites, this decline has benefitted, and offered more opportunities for, the non-Arab states, namely Iran, Turkey, and Israel. Egypt in particular has seen its power and influence in the Middle East recede.

The final panel reviewed the situation in Afghanistan and Pakistan. Brian Katulis began by highlighting the impact of the surge of additional U.S. forces in Afghanistan in 2010. He said that while there have been some positive results, it remains uncertain whether the gains will be sustainable because the conflict "is quite complicated." He stated that the political and development components have lagged and remain the "weakest links." The Afghan government is an obvious problem, but Katulis also observed that in his travels in the country, he had not seen the tangible results of the $50 billion that the U.S. government has invested in development aid. He also noted that building the Afghan security forces has been a "much harder process" than it was in Iraq. Meanwhile Pakistan, according to Katulis, "remains stuck in past," and he believed that Pakistan would become more of a focal point of U.S. action over the subsequent two to three years, not militarily, but in assisting the United States with its development and security challenges in an attempt to bring more stability to the region.

Stephen D. Biddle argued that U.S. counterinsurgency doctrine, which emphasizes capacity building, has been "directly unhelpful" in Afghanistan because significant elements in the government there have "malign intentions." By improving the capacity of these duplicitous actors, the Americans are making them "more efficient predators." He said that while there is no evidence that the Afghan people prefer the Taliban to a "nonpredatory government," at the moment, people feel that they have no alternatives. Biddle's blunt assessment was that "if this continues, we will lose the war, regardless of how aggressively we pursue the security part of our strategy, regardless of how well it's implemented, and regardless of how many troops are tied up in doing it." He stressed that to make any progress, the United States has to find a way to shut off the flow of money into the "malign actor networks."

In reevaluating U.S. policy, Paul R. Pillar said that America needs to address the fundamental question of whether it should be undertaking a counterinsurgency effort in Afghanistan, which he sees as engaged in a "civil war." According to Pillar, a military victory over the Taliban is not "a key" to protecting Americans from international terrorism, as the Taliban's main interest is in the political and social order of Afghanistan. If the primary U.S. goal in the region is a more stable Pakistan, counterinsurgency in Afghanistan is not the best approach to achieving it. Pillar averred, however, that Pakistan is "a very important player" in the regional diplomacy and must be more involved in regional stability efforts, as well as delinked from the Taliban. He advised that the United States needs to encourage more regional engagement and be open to potential power-sharing peace arrangements in Afghanistan.

Hassan Abbas opened his presentation by declaring that "very clearly," the United States is "still in search of a comprehensive and sustainable policy toward Pakistan." He stated that there is a disconnect between the two countries, based largely on mistrust. As he sees it, the issue of nuclear security is the number-one foreign policy concern for the United States in Pakistan, with the second being militancy in the tribal areas. Abbas reviewed five areas of interaction: development aid; engagement with the Pakistani military; U.S. support for democracy; U.S. help for Pakistan in times of crisis, including the 2010 floods; and U.S. drone attacks in Pakistan. Points of emphasis missing from the relationship, according to Abbas, are linkage to civil society actors in Pakistan; the need for Pakistani police reform; efforts toward de-radicalization; and the lack of American understanding about why Pakistan formulates its policies based on its fixation on India.

*　　*　　*

Even in the wake of the seismic events of early 2011—the "Arab Spring," Fatah and Hamas reaching a tentative agreement, and the killing of Osama bin Laden in Pakistan—the vast majority of issues raised at the conference in November 2010 are ongoing. Some have become even more complicated. Indeed, in Egypt after the fall of the Mubarak government, a Pew Global Attitudes survey found that 54 percent of Egyptians would like to see the peace agreement with Israel annulled, with only 36 percent in favor of maintaining it.[7] The Middle East remains "in transition," and this book documents the complexity of that evolution.

EDITORIAL NOTE

All chapters in this book were originally oral presentations, most delivered with no prepared script. The talks have been transcribed and lightly edited for publication, but they still retain the flavor of spoken presentations. False starts have been silently omitted, as have introductory and concluding words of thanks to the audience and the Middle East Institute. Annotation has been added where speakers have referenced specific publications or documents and to clarify points in the text. Full footnoted referencing of the many events in recent Middle East history mentioned by the speakers is beyond the scope of this work. Readers are encouraged to consult the publications by the speakers that are listed under their biographies in the "Contributors" section.

In the discussion sections at the end of each part, only a few of the audience questioners were identifiable, so the names are not given. Moderator interjections and guidance not directly related to the subject matter have also been omitted.

ACKNOWLEDGMENTS

This book owes much, on multiple fronts, to the efforts of Kate Seeyle, vice president of the Middle East Institute, who was the point person for organizing the conference on which it is based, and who worked closely with Marine Corps University Press in developing this publication. The president of MEI, Ambassador Wendy J. Chamberlin, has been an enthusiastic supporter of this project and provided the preface. Elisha

---

7 The polling in Egypt was conducted March 24 through April 7, 2011. Pew Research Center, "Egyptians Embrace Revolt Leaders, Religious Parties and Military, As Well," April 25, 2011, http://pewglobal.org /files/2011/04/Pew-Global-Attitudes-Egypt-Report-FINAL-April-25-2011.pdf. On this issue, see also the thoughts of conference contributor David Makovsky, "Reviewing Egypt's Gains from its Peace Treaty with Israel," Washington Institute for Near East Policy, Policy Watch #1772, March 7, 2011, http:// www.washingtoninstitute.org/templateC05.php?CID=3322. For Israel's official views on the Spring 2011 developments, including the Fatah–Hamas agreement, see the interview with Michael Oren, Israeli ambassador to the United States, "Hamas–Included Government May Hinder Peace Talks," NPR *Morning Edition*, May 5, 2011, http://www.npr.org/2011/05/05/136011913/palestinian-unity-government-worries-israeli-ambassador-oren. Robert Malley commented in his presentation in this volume that the United States needed to stop seeing Palestinian reconciliation "as an obstacle to peace, but rather as one of the preconditions for peace."

Meyer, the MEI director of programs and communications, and intern Kylie Beard also contributed.

At Marine Corps University Press, editorial colleagues Shawn H. Vreeland, Andrea L. Connell, and James M. Caiella helped proof the manuscript, as did intern Abbi N. Molzhan. Robert A. Kocher designed the book.

U.S. President Barack Obama talks with Israeli Prime Minister Benjamin Netanyahu outside of the Oval Office after their meeting on May 20, 2011, in Washington, DC. (AP Images/Rex Features/Official White House Photo by Pete Souza)

Part One

America's Middle East Policy in the Second Half of the Obama Term

CHAPTER ONE

EFFORTS IN ISRAELI-PALESTINIAN MEDIATION

DAVID MAKOVSKY

Having reached the midway point of this term, it is now a logical time to evaluate whether the [Barack H.] Obama administration's efforts in the Israeli-Palestinian mediation are starting to bear fruit, and to look ahead at prospects for the future.[1]

The Obama administration inherited a difficult set of conditions in 2009. The [George W.] Bush administration's effort to define the Israeli-Palestinian endgame up front in what is known as the Annapolis process had come up short. Israeli Prime Minister Ehud Olmert faced corruption charges and was ultimately forced to resign. During the final months of 2008, promising back-channel efforts with Palestinian President [Mahmoud] Abbas succeeded in narrowing territorial differences to a little over 4 percent, but the process was not durable. It went up in smoke with Olmert's resignation and the Gaza war, which raged from late 2008 to just before the Obama inauguration.

As President Obama entered office, a very different political landscape emerged between Israelis and Palestinians. A new [Benjamin] Netanyahu government was formed [in Israel] in the February 2009 election. The new administration was not keen on picking up the Annapolis process where Olmert and Abbas had left off. Abbas, for his part, found himself cornered. He did not trust Netanyahu, and he felt trapped by Obama's call for a complete settlement freeze in the spring of 2009. As Abbas has stated in multiple public interviews and in a conversation we had together in Ramallah this summer in his office, he had never insisted in the past on a freeze being a pre-

---

1 For links to Makovsky's writings and presentations that deal with many of the issues addressed in this presentation, see his site at the Washington Institute for Near East Policy, http://www.washington institute.org/templateC10.php?CID=6.

condition for talks during the previous negotiations with Olmert. Nor had [Yasir] Arafat made this a precondition in negotiations with [Yitzhak] Rabin and [Ehud] Barak. In several interviews over the last year, Abbas has blamed the United States for installing a settlement freeze as its own precondition, although to be fair to the Obama administration, the U.S. never actually called it a precondition. Abbas feels Obama, in his words, got him "up a tree without a ladder." He made it clear that he could not be outflanked and appear to be less pro-Palestinian than President Obama.

While the U.S. was correct in pinpointing settlements as a major irritant that needed to be dealt with, setting the bar as high as a complete freeze led even the opponents of the settlements in Israel to be silent. There were no rallies in Israel saying "Say Yes to Obama," as existed during Mr. [Edward P.] Djerejian's term [in the George H.W. Bush administration] when they said "Say Yes to Baker" [U.S. Secretary of State James A. Baker III]. Once Netanyahu had already said at that moment that he was willing to not geographically expand settlements—this may seem to some of you to be splitting of hairs, but it turned out to be a huge distinction—the administration could have taken the position of "no expansion of settlements," and I think we would have saved over a year. Had we taken this alternate position, the issue would have been defused, and final-status negotiations would not have been prejudged. Neither my colleague Rob Malley nor myself are huge fans of settlements. Yet I agree with what Malley told the *New York Times* on October 5 regarding the U.S. approach to settlements: "The original sin was putting so much emphasis on this, an issue we could not resolve." He added, "We spent the whole year trying to undo the damage of that step."[2]

Indeed, something odd would transpire. With the bar set so high, the Abbas government rejected the U.S.-endorsed settlement moratorium of November 2009 as falling short of what it truly needed. Yet by August 2010, what was insignificant the previous fall had suddenly become indispensable. So we have gone from the inconsequential to the indispensable. Abbas insisted that the settlement moratorium must continue.

Moreover, 9 of the 10 months in which the moratorium was in place were utterly wasted. I think if you speak to Palestinians privately, they will admit that. The Arab states did not come through with their promise to match Israeli steps toward the Palestinians with steps of their own toward Israel.

2 Mark Landler, "Risks and Advantages in U.S. Effort in Mideast," *New York Times*, October 5, 2010, http://www.nytimes.com/2010/10/06/world/middleeast/06diplo.html.

All this in turn was then utilized by Israelis as a reason not to extend the moratorium beyond September 2010, saying that the whole period had been wasted anyway. The 2009 to August 2010 period was an opportunity utterly lost, a loss magnified by the fact that developments on the ground in the West Bank were actually improving. Economic growth in the West Bank was 9 percent last year, according to the International Monetary Fund. This is at a time of global recession. (Parenthetically, and a subject maybe for Q&A, the economic assistance to the Palestinians, which has been prominent in the Obama administration—the U.S. is the biggest giver to the Palestinians—that could come under pressure now, I fear, with a Republican-led House.)

There were problems, certainly, on the Israeli side, too. Israeli Foreign Minister Avigdor Lieberman disparaged his own premier's peacemaking efforts, saying peace will not come in this or the next generation. By the way, the one month of the moratorium where the Palestinians agreed to direct talks—this past September—they lacked a bold focus on territory in those negotiations, which could have forced the Palestinians to put the moratorium issue in a wider context. I think Israel has to think about some soul-searching as well.

So how [do the parties] avoid further missed opportunities and ensure that the settlement issue no longer overshadows the issue of peace negotiations, or issues of symptom no longer overwhelm the issue of curing the problem? It would be a bitter irony if the current situation indeed continued.

On the one hand, Netanyahu has reached some degree of success with President Obama this summer. Having never paid Netanyahu any compliments in the past, Obama came out of the July 6 [2010] meeting at the Oval Office and said, "I think he wants peace. I think he is willing to take risks for peace."[3] Having reversed course and endorsed the two-state solution in a policy speech in June 2009, Netanyahu apparently confided in Obama about his specific end point in reaching a two-state solution. The fact that he wants to hold peace talks directly with Abbas could be a sign of seriousness that he does not want the talks ensnared in mid-level foot-dragging.

While Netanyahu may have successfully shared an objective with the U.S. and the Palestinians, he has not demonstrated a strategy to overcome his domestic constraints

---

3 Office of the White House Press Secretary, "Remarks by President Obama and Prime Minister Netanyahu of Israel in Joint Press Availability," July 6, 2010 (http://www.whitehouse.gov/the-press-office/remarks-president-obama-and-prime-minister-netanyahu-israel-joint-press-availabilit).

and reach the ultimate objective. Herein lies the Netanyahu paradox. On one hand, Netanyahu fears a premature fracturing of the Israeli right, whereby Lieberman will attack any preliminary concessions and force Netanyahu, in his view, to lose his electoral base. To this end, Netanyahu hopes to conduct negotiations in such an intimate setting with Abbas that he will be forced to make decisions only at the final moment, culminating in one big decision point. Until then, he seeks to preserve his political capital and his coalition. Yet this could be at the expense of Abbas, and this presumes that it requires the Middle East to operate under laboratory-like conditions, with hermetically sealed rooms and a friction-free period during the entire duration of the peace talks. The Middle East does not operate under laboratory conditions, and therefore, one may never reach the point where the political capital can finally be spent.

The paradox of Netanyahu's approach of making one massive decision at the end and avoiding all decisions along the way is that it could invite the very outcome he seeks to avoid, which is an Obama peace plan. If the U.S. is convinced that the parties will not be able to reach a decision due to the political wear and tear they will experience along the way, Obama may be prompted to put forward a plan for the peace talks in order to force that very big decision. Indeed, traditionally, U.S. plans work best in either of two scenarios: either as a bridge over a river (not over an ocean, like the [William J.] Clinton parameters of December 2000), or as a walk-away strategy for the U.S., hoping to stir public debate in each society. Those who favor an Obama plan want a third outcome: viewing it as a potential lever, here and now, as an instrument for breakthrough. Yet as we know, this is uncertain.

It seems the main way to avoid this go-for-broke U.S. approach is to ensure that the Netanyahu government is broadened to include the Kadima Party, which has a critical 28 seats in the 120-member Knesset. With a broadened government, there would be sturdier support for a strategy to reach a two-state solution. Whether it is a policy of the U.S.-led approach or the politics of a broadened government in Israel, these are the two possible policy options for the coming year. It is clear that if there is no broadened government, I think the prospects of an Obama peace plan shoot way up.

Even under the best of circumstances, it will be difficult for both peoples to solve all the differences. There has been little conditioning of the societal landscape of both societies in dealing with the two narrative issues of this conflict: Jerusalem and refugees. Both issues cut to the self-definition of the parties, given how intertwined the issues of religion and nationalism have become. Yet it is important to remember that the territorial differences between the parties were narrowed during the Olmert-Abbas negotiations, and these differences of 4 percent are indeed bridgeable.

Today marks the 15th anniversary of the killing of Yitzhak Rabin, the iconic ex-general who gave his life for peace.[4] This month is also the sixth anniversary of the death of Yasir Arafat, who personified Palestinian nationalism. The tragedy of this conflict should not be allowed to continue for another generation, let alone a generation after that. Based on the twin pillars of dignity and security, we should not allow the past to bury the future any longer in the Middle East.

---

4 See David Makovsky, "Why I Still Miss Yitzhak Rabin," ForeignPolicy.com, November 3, 2010, http://www.foreignpolicy.com/articles/2010/11/03/why_I_still_miss_yitzhak_rabin.

CHAPTER TWO

Iraq: The Jury is Still Out

Joost R. Hiltermann

We are at a stage where we have seen seven years of an American presence in Iraq and yet no clear way out. Yet there could be a way out, and much will depend on what is happening in Baghdad these very days. There is no question, however, that even if Iraq succeeds, it will have been at a terrible human cost, and of course a cost in treasure as well.

The United States entered Iraq in 2003 and created a *tabula rasa* without a plan for rebuilding, leaving this essentially to the military. Originally, the idea was to leave this to former Iraqi exiles who would come back and be greeted and welcomed by the population and accepted as their leaders. The [George W.] Bush administration was congenitally opposed to state building, nation building. It had made this very clear. But because [it became apparent that] the former exiles could not play this role, it was suddenly faced with the task of rebuilding Iraq. There was no plan, because this was not expected. There was no coordination. There was no continuity. In the end, there was much corruption.

Three vacuums were created in those first days of 2003:

• A political vacuum, by removing the regime—perhaps rightly so—but replacing it with a group of people who were former exiles and former expats (at least the majority of them) and who had no local grounding or support, no local constituencies.

• A security vacuum, by disbanding the entire military apparatus. Parts of it probably should have been disbanded, but the entire army was sent packing. It had never expressed any solidarity with the regime, and in fact because Saddam Hussein distrusted his army, he had created a number of parallel institutions to protect him from it.

• A managerial vacuum, through the de-Baathification process, which sent home a lot of capable bureaucrats who were judged on their membership in a party rather than on their actual conduct during the years of the regime.

The results of these "original sins" were polarization and violence and, over time, sectarian war. The January 2005 elections, much heralded as the first indicator of democratic progress in Iraq, aggravated the situation because the results led to the exclusion of one particular community—not just a political party, but a community—which then was also excluded from the very important process of drafting the new constitution. That constitution, which eventually was accepted in a referendum, had very controversial clauses about a federal structure in Iraq that was based on an original notion pushed very much by the Kurds during their years of exile. The federal structure was premised on the existence of a Kurdistan region, and also on the possibility of new regions emerging in the rest of Iraq, an issue that remains highly controversial to this very day.

A sectarian war evolved in the summer of 2005, not, as President Bush likes to say, in February 2006. It happened after many attempts at jump-starting such a war (just as we are seeing similar attempts today). It turned into a cycle of vengeance from the moment the government that was elected in January 2005 took power in May–June 2005.

The "surge" [in 2008] ended this. That is also a controversial point. I think that militarily, the surge was successful in dampening violence in the areas where it mattered the most, especially Baghdad. But the surge also had—and I think it's a factor often overlooked—a psychological impact. It showed Iraqis that the United States was still committed to Iraq. They had started to doubt this. It showed especially to the Sunni community that the United States was willing to stand up to Iran, because from the

Sunni perspective, the government in Baghdad was a Shi'ite Islamist government that was a proxy for Iran. So by coming in with extra forces and saving the Sunnis, essentially, they saw it as a recalibration of American power that would give them a way back into Iraq and to curb Iranian influence.

That psychological impact is starting to peter out now as we see that the Ayad Allawi list may not make it into the next government. Allawi is now speaking about going into opposition. His constituency, which is largely Sunni Arab, may not go into opposition. It may revert to insurgency. We will have to wait and see if this scenario comes to pass.

Today, the three vacuums I mentioned persist, but in diminished form. We have security forces that have filled the security vacuum, but they remain weak, and most importantly, they lack cohesion. This could become a problem if and when political negotiations break down, for example, over government formation.

This will become especially acute when United States forces withdraw by the end of next year. What will come next? In the absence of American forces, the United States says it will continue to be heavily invested and engaged in Iraq through the strategic framework agreement that the Bush administration signed at the end of 2008.[1] But the question is, will Congress fund it? Congress seems to think that Iraq is a very rich country with huge revenues from oil, but Iraq is *potentially* a rich country. It is at least a decade away from reaping the fruits from its resources, from its natural wealth. In the coming 10 years, when it starts developing its oil wealth, it will need all the revenues to reconstruct the country, which is really in terrible shape at this moment (minus the Kurdistan region).

The other question is, will the Iraqis want it? Will the Iraqis want a close partnership with the United States? I think that will very much depend on the composition of the next government. Is it going to be a government that is leaning toward Iran? If that's the case, a close partnership with the United States would become highly problematic. If it is a more broadly based government, then I think such a partnership would be very possible. We have to wait and see.

---

1 Office of the White House Press Secretary, "Declaration of Principles for a Long-Term Relationship of Cooperation and Friendship between the Republic of Iraq and the United States of America," November 27, 2007, http://georgewbush-whitehouse.archives.gov/news/releases/2007/11/20071126-11.html.

If in fact the next Iraqi government is not inclusive and tends toward the pro-Iranian side of things, the United States may leave Iraq without any tangible gain and with a net loss—that Iraq will have entered into the Iranian sphere of influence. That means that the future of Iraq will very much depend on the state of U.S.-Iranian relations. If there is a settlement between Iran and the United States over the nuclear question, then things in Iraq could well look up. If not, then Iraq may become the battleground.

But if Iraq is left in peace, if it is given the time to develop its political institutions, it will also have the time to develop natural antibodies to external influence, including Iranian influence.

To sum up this historical period, the U.S. tenure is marked by occupation much more than liberation. There was liberation, but it was not only liberation, it was mostly—especially in the Iraqi view—occupation. It was imposition rather than respect for sovereignty, repeatedly. It was excellent people doing excellent stuff, but in the end, with very little to show for it. American timetables dictated the pace of Iraqi developments. There was disorganization, discontinuity, and a disconnect between the outsiders and the insiders—the outsiders being American forces, American diplomats, and the former exiles and expats on the one side, and ordinary Iraqis on the other, and politicians bred in Iraq itself who had never left.

There was also expediency over vision and institution building. You can mention the police—no one even focused on the police in the first few years after 2003. It was a key element. Electricity was ignored by and large, and then fixes were attempted through patchwork reconstruction of power stations, but there was never any strategy or plan. It was all tactics, no strategy.

Finally, the U.S. military learned its lessons much better than the civilian side. But in the end, state building is not a military job, and the military is leaving. So what is next? Here is my advice. I would say don't smother Iraq. Allow for a close partnership, but let it be a partnership. Allow Iraqi nationalism to push out external actors. Don't start building consulates in Najaf, which is not in the plans right now, simply because the Iranians have built a consulate in Najaf. It would be the wrong reaction.

Help build key institutions. The Iraqis remain highly dependent on the United States for expertise, for advice and assistance. They need independent institutions, especially a strong judiciary. Of course they also still need help with security forces. They need a stronger parliament. Most of all, they need advice.

Condition aid with these objectives in mind. Don't just turn a blind eye on abuse of power, on human rights violations. Ordinary Iraqis take note.

Do not induct Iraq in a struggle against Iran. The result would be an Iraqi collapse.

Finally, pay attention to Iraqi priorities. In the long term, these may be the most beneficial to U.S. interests in the region.

CHAPTER THREE

Taking Stock of U.S. Policy Toward Iran

Suzanne Maloney

I t seems to be a very useful moment to take stock of U.S. policy toward Iran, not simply because the conference is timed so nicely at the very midterm point of the [Barack H.] Obama administration's first and/or final term; not simply because of the fact that we have now seen just about a year of each portion of the Obama administration's dual-track policy toward Iran; but also because it appears that we may be on the verge of another round of dialogue between the Iranians and the international community on their nuclear program.

The Obama administration came into office after a unique, tumultuous, and poorly understood U.S.–Iranian relationship during the George W. Bush administration, an administration that saw both historic engagement, unprecedented contact between high-level Iranian and high-level U.S. officials on issues of immediate concern (that being Afghanistan in the aftermath of 9/11), and then an unprecedented period of almost no diplomatic contact between the two sides because of an unprecedented decision by the Bush administration to abstain and dismiss any prospects for diplomacy with Iran, obviously informed by the initial euphoria over the invasion of Iraq.

Obama made engagement with Iran a priority in his campaign, somewhat surprisingly, and even against some opposition from within his own party as well as opposition from the other side. The change that the Obama administration promised in its policy toward Iran appears to be much more in terms of style than in substance. Gone are the references to carrot-and-stick diplomacy, replaced by the phrase "dual-track." During the first year, the Obama administration promised engagement. What we saw of engagement has largely been deemed a failure by the prevailing conventional wisdom here in Washington. The broad overtures that the administration launched—the Nowruz message,[1] the apparent letters that we have seen reports of from the president to his counterpart, the Supreme Leader Ali Khamenei—received very little in the way of a productive response. The one attempt at specific negotiations on the nuclear program, which resulted in a preliminary agreement on a modest confidence-building measure that would have resulted in the refueling of the Tehran Research Reactor [TRR] and the removal of a significant proportion of Iran's low-enriched uranium from the country, collapsed just weeks after the agreement.

The lack of reciprocity from the Iranian side confirmed initial skepticism within the administration about the utility of engagement. The 2009 election turmoil within Iran, and the rise of the first really indigenous and legitimate opposition within Iran to the regime, killed the prospects for engagement, both as a paradigm—the idea of rapprochement as a possibility with a regime that was engaged with such distasteful actions toward its own population—and as a tactic, largely because it became politically impossible to reach out in any really dramatic way in the aftermath of the June 2009 elections.

About a year ago, the Obama administration began shifting, as in fact candidate Obama had signaled that he would, toward pressure, toward the coercive part of U.S. diplomacy. It took a while. It took a surprising six months for an administration with a considerable honeymoon period in Europe, and with the assistance of a "reset" in the relationship with Russia, to obtain another United Nations Security Council resolution. Resolution 1929,[2] approved in June of this year, has proven to be the most effective, surprisingly, not only because of the terms that it contained, which include an arms embargo (a little-noticed but very important provision for Iran's long-term future as a conventional military threat), but also because the language within that resolution served as a platform for follow-on measures by "like-minded states"—Europeans, Australians, Japanese, and others—which have begun to unveil a series of unilateral finan-

---

1 Office of the White House Press Secretary, "Videotaped Remarks by the President in Celebration of Nowruz," March 20, 2009 (http://www.whitehouse.gov/the-press-office/videotaped-remarks-president-celebration-nowruz); "Remarks of President Obama Marking Nowruz," March 20, 2010 (http://www.whitehouse.gov/the-press-office/remarks-president-obama-marking-nowruz).

2 United Nations Security Council Resolution 1929, adopted June 9, 2010 (http://daccess-dds-ny.un.org/doc/UNDOC/GEN/N10/396/79/PDF/N1039679.pdf).

cial restrictions on Iran. All these measures, in concert with a stepped-up effort by the U.S. Treasury to continue to close the international financial system to the Iranians, have had a real impact, as has congressional action, with a range of new unilateral and third-party sanctions and moral suasion on companies that has forced many companies to leave Iran.

The implication at this point, when you talk with U.S. officials, is that sanctions are working. We have the much-vaunted leverage that we have been seeking for many years. But—and of course there is always a "but" when Iran is concerned—it remains unclear whether the sort of economic pain that the sanctions are causing—the difficulties in getting letters of credit, the difficulties that we know that traders and businessmen are experiencing in going about their day-to-day business and transactions—it is difficult to understand at this stage whether or not that economic price is high enough yet to force Iran to change its nuclear calculations. It remains unclear how China—a key actor—will act, unconstrained by some of the bans on energy investment that the Europeans have now adopted.

It is not clear precisely how the main factor that has impacted U.S. policy toward Iran—Iran's internal dynamics—has been impacted by these measures to date. I am going to speak a few words on this issue because what happens within Iran is the most consequential element of U.S. policy. It is the piece that we understand so poorly and that we have almost no ability to influence in a positive fashion.

There are three or four big political earthquakes underway within Iran today. The first is the splintering of the conservatives, an inevitable feature of Iranian politics, which have always been very much fragmented and always included a considerable degree of political competition within the boundaries of the red lines of the regime. As soon as the conservatives had begun to eliminate the reformist rivals from the day-to-day political scene, they began feuding among themselves. It has become particularly salient because [Iranian President Mahmoud] Ahmadinejad is something like the "tea party" of Iran. He comes from a certain ideological perspective, he shares interests and cultural norms with the traditional conservatives of the Iranian regime, and yet he is radical and provocative. He is eclectic in his ideology. This is someone who advocated for women to enter soccer stadiums and for an end to some of the cultural segregation. He is unorthodox, and as a result, he unnerves even those who share many of his interests and his aims. So this factor has complicated the Iranian internal scene, and it has complicated U.S. diplomacy. The conventional wisdom is that the TRR agreement concluded last fall collapsed as a result of some of the internal sniping within the regime against Ahmadinejad.

The other main political factors, which I won't go into in great depth, that I think are worth noting and are going to have a major impact on the prospects for U.S. diplomacy are, first, the elimination of the left wing. The reformists are still present in very small numbers in the Iranian parliament, but they are no longer the sort of force within day-to-day politics that they have been since the dawn of the revolution. They were the heirs to the Marxist ideology that was present at the time in the 1970s, and they have transformed themselves ideologically and politically, but they have always been an important feature of Iranian politics. At this stage, they have largely been neutralized as a result of the repression that has ensued since the election turmoil last year.

The other important political trends to note are the sidelining of [Ali Akbar Hashemi] Rafsanjani, the political godfather of Iran, someone with a somewhat pragmatic posture who has been able to influence Iranian politics in that direction at key moments in its prior political history, and of course the rise of the Revolutionary Guard, a trend which I think is very poorly understood at this stage but obviously quite salient to Iran's policy.

What comes next? So far, Iran is behaving predictably. Under economic pressure, the Iranians are adopting painful economic reforms, including the change to a vast subsidy program, which has been an important feature of Iran's ability to buy off its own population. It is a very dangerous move for the regime to undertake, and it remains to be seen whether it can be done successfully without social upheaval, but if it is successful, it will blunt some of the impact of sanctions.

The Iranians are also behaving predictably in the sense that they are dangling dialogue before the international community. I think the most likely outcome of the upcoming talks, if in fact they do proceed, is that there is a possibility of achieving some sort of modified version of the failed Tehran Research Reactor proposal that was put forward last fall, that the Iranians continue to trumpet, including in their Tehran declaration signed with the Turks and Brazilians last spring. Clearly, this is something that they want, for a variety of reasons, and it is clearly something that can serve as a sort of confidence-building measure.

The difficulty, of course, is that we can expect the Iranians to renege on or renegotiate any agreement that they are likely to conclude. The difficulty beyond that is simply in trying to create the kind of momentum from what this side at least will perceive as a very modest gesture. To create momentum, to really get to the crux of the nuclear issue, both enrichment and whatever other confidence-building measures can be designed would need to be ones that would in fact ensure that the international community has sufficient transparency and clarity on the Iranian program to avoid a nuclear breakout.

There is a great deal of talk these days about war in Washington, which I would credit more to pot-stirring journalists than I think to any dialogue from either the administration or from the Israelis. It is a persistent backdrop, though, and it is a problematic one, because the more likely and more unfortunate scenario that we may see if in fact negotiations are not successful is an Iran that looks something like the Iraq of the 1990s—impoverished, more isolated, hollowed out, and more radicalized as a result of all of these trends. To avoid this, we need to look at the upcoming negotiations and take steps that in fact are likely to create the kind of positive momentum that will at least enable both sides to move forward beyond any initial agreement.

CHAPTER FOUR

Connecting the Dots: A Comprehensive Strategy for a Broader Middle East

Edward P. Djerejian

I accepted this difficult assignment to try and connect the dots in the Middle East, which is really a mission impossible. First, I think as President [Barack H.] Obama moves into this phase of his mandate, there truly is—and has been—a need for a coherent and comprehensive strategy toward the broader Middle East. The administration needs to connect the dots. This is not only this administration; every administration needs to connect the dots in the broader Middle East in order for American foreign policy to be truly effective. We have had successes, and we have had many failures, but the basic tenets of U.S. foreign policy still apply: we remain the premier economic, military, and diplomatic power.

Yet the projection of our power is limited. Militarily, we are overstretched. We have the endgame in Iraq; we have ongoing military action and war in Afghanistan. The threat scenario in the Korean peninsula is always there. There are asymmetrical challenges in Yemen, Somalia, and Iran. Also, as is painfully evident and was reflected in our elections here, U.S. economic power is limited. The current economic crisis necessitates coordination of economic policy with other nations. In addition, U.S. diplomatic power will be seriously limited when we cannot obtain the support of other key countries. Building *real* coalitions—not fake coalitions, but real coalitions—is very important for the Obama administration.

Obviously, we will act unilaterally when our vital interests are threatened, as in 9/11 and the first war in Afghanistan, which was quite successful until we turned our backs. But the basic thrust of our approach now should be to work with allies and coalitions.

Suzanne Maloney mentioned that in Iran, what Russia and China do will be very important in terms of sanctions and the whole thrust of our policy toward Iran. In 1991 in the Gulf War, we were successful in building a real coalition, [both] international and of Arabs. We need strong coalitions in the war against terrorism. I don't like the phrase "war against terrorism." I think it's a false slogan. I think it is an ongoing struggle. There is not going to be an Iwo Jima victory with planting the flag and saying we won the war on terrorism. It will be a continual struggle.

We need a strategic dialogue with our adversaries. This is one thing that President Obama has started his administration with, which I applaud—the need for the United States to engage its adversaries in a tough-minded dialogue; not talk for the sake of talk, but a tough-minded dialogue. That is certainly the case today with North Korea, but certainly with Syria and Iran in the Middle East as well. Yes, this means dealing with authoritarian regimes, but I find it an incredible anomaly, and having been ambassador to Syria at a very difficult time under the [Ronald W.] Reagan and [George H.W.] Bush administrations, that we do not have a U.S. ambassador in Damascus. It is ridiculous for the United States to consider posting an ambassador in an adversarial state, or a state we have problems with, as a political concession to that country. It is delusionary.

Our diplomacy must be based on both our values and our interests. I think one of the things I would like to see the Obama administration do is move from conflict management—constantly putting out the fires—to a more substantive move toward conflict resolution. As David Makovsky has mentioned on the Arab-Israeli conflict, that is critical. As President Bill Clinton mentioned last night at the dinner, this is the one seminal political issue that goes all over the Muslim world: the Palestinian issue and the Arab–Israeli conflict. Any American president that can make headway on that deserves full support from all the constituencies in our country.

We cannot talk about what we have discussed on this panel without putting into perspective our situation here at home, and the incredibly difficult economic situation we have, with the debt and the deficit. I think many of you know of Niall Ferguson, the historian at Harvard University, who has written that national decline has historically begun with a debt explosion, ending in a reduction in available revenues for the army, the navy, the air force of superpowers. This was obviously the case with Hapsburg Spain, the Ottoman Empire, the British. Despite our view of American exceptionalism, this can happen to us. So the president has to confront the incredible economic challenges we have nationally, and that will also affect what he feels that he will be able to do internationally, especially in the broader Middle East.

We should not only be fixated on our own economic situation. The economic situation in the Middle East is very, very difficult. More than half of the 300 million residents of the Middle East are under 25 years of age. There is already a high unemployment rate of 15 percent. The Middle East must create 80 million new jobs in the next five years just to keep apace of its own demographics. Unemployment is a problem affecting all 22 member states of the Arab League, but it is conspicuously a youth issue: 50 percent of the jobless are under 25, roughly double the world average, and women in the Middle East have an especially difficult time finding jobs.

The total expenditure on conflicts in the Middle East in the last six decades has exceeded $3 trillion. In fact, the Middle East is the world's most militarized region. How much does the Middle East spend on education? The per capita expenditure of the region's 22 nations on education has shrunk in the last 15 years from 20 percent to 10 percent. Education is critical because education and the development of the economies of these countries will stabilize and provide sustainable security in the Middle East. The threat of extremism and radicalism in the Middle East comes from within. The wonderful military we have, and our own diplomatic service, and the Fifth Fleet in Bahrain, will not be able to reverse a situation when radicals take over and the threat is a crumbling from within.

On Afghanistan, this is President Obama's war. It is a war in which there is within the administration still an inner debate as to what the right approach will be, especially next year [2011] when the president has pledged to begin the withdrawal of American forces. But when the Obama administration looks at the Afghan war, it is too myopic to be looking at the war in Afghanistan from the so-called AfPak perspective. You have to put India into the equation. One of the major reasons that Pakistan hedges its bets—

especially the ISI [Inter-Services Intelligence]—in Afghanistan is because it still considers, and the Pakistani military still considers, India as the major national threat to Pakistan, and they do not want India outflanking Pakistan through Afghanistan. It will continue to hedge its bets as long as the issue of Pakistan-India relations is not being addressed more directly. That, of course—when I talked of going from conflict management to conflict resolution—involves the issue of Kashmir.

So I would urge the administration to think more strategically when it looks at South Asia, and connect the dots when it looks at the broader Middle East, along the lines of the issues that I have raised.

Let me end on the Arab–Israeli perspective. In my eyes, there cannot be an effective American approach toward conflict resolution in the Arab-Israeli framework unless our approach is more comprehensive. As David Makovsky mentioned, because the Israeli–Palestinian talks are so fragile, any outside power or group has too high a probability of sabotaging those talks, be it Hamas, be it Hezbollah, be it Iran. Therefore, our approach toward Arab–Israeli conflict resolution should be more comprehensive. We did that in Madrid. When I was in government, we had a strong foreign-policy president, a strong secretary of state, and we had a comprehensive view of bringing the parties together. We brought the parties together. We brought a Likud prime minister, Yitzhak Shamir, to the table in Madrid in direct, face-to-face negotiations with all its Arab neighbors. It can be done. Of course the historical context is different, then and now, but it can be done. But you have to connect the dots. Syria has to be part of the equation. [Hamas leader] Khaled Meshaal lives in Damascus. Syria has influence in Lebanon and on Hezbollah, as does Iran. So approaching Israeli–Palestinian talks strictly in the Israeli-Palestinian context, in my eyes, is a mistake.

I just want to state something that I feel very strongly. I have heard Secretary of State Hillary Clinton mention this, and the president has mentioned this. I like it because it accords with my own analysis. The three major factors that make me very anxious about the Israeli–Palestinian equation are demographics, topography and technology, and ideology.

I have served on the Arab side; I have served in Israel. The imperative of a two-state solution, so that there can be a state called Israel, living in peace and security with its Arab neighbors, to me is compelling. I think a one-state solution would certainly be the end of the Israeli state as we know it. I don't think it is a viable option. But the two-state solution, every year that goes by, the two-state solution is at risk. On the issue of demography, the Arab populations are multiplying at a much faster rate, and in the next 10 or 20 years, the Jewish population in that part of the world will become increasingly small. Both within Israel and outside of Israel, the Arab population will grow at a faster rate.

As for military technology and topography, President Clinton mentioned this last night at the dinner. Today, topography—land, occupying the land—is not as essential as it was in 1973 in the Yom Kippur War, where we still had armored battles. With GPS [global positioning] systems, ballistic missiles, with Hezbollah reportedly in possession of 40,000 rockets, there can be devastation done by military technology. So the occupation of the land, per se, is not a guarantor of security.

Lastly, there is ideology. That is on both sides of the equation. Islamic radicalism feeds to a great extent on the irresolution of the Palestinian issue. It is not the only issue—there will be terrorism even if there is an Arab–Israeli peace settlement—but it feeds on it. In Israel, again as President Clinton mentioned last night, it was an Israeli young man, an extremist, who killed Yitzhak Rabin.

So with these three compelling factors, I would hope that President Obama will live up to the vision that he expressed at the beginning of his administration and have the political will and courage to go for an Israeli–Palestinian and an Israeli–Lebanese settlement.

CHAPTER FIVE

Discussion of America's Middle East Policy

Moderated by Barbara K. Bodine

Question: My question is for Suzanne Maloney. It picks up on the importance of Mr. [Edward P.] Djerejian's stress on the need for engagement with adversaries. I hear voices of people who have considerable expertise on Iran, including lots of Iranian–Americans, saying that we should not reward the current authoritarian and repressive government in Iran with engagement with the United States. Would you comment on this?

Suzanne Maloney: I understand and sympathize with that critique, but I don't agree with it, simply because I don't think we have the luxury of choosing our adversaries. Those of us who were always supporters of engagement have made the argument that this regime can behave in a pragmatic fashion and pursue its own interests in terms of foreign policy. Obviously, [Ali] Khamenei has at various points in the Islamic Republic's history taken decisions that appear to counter the basic ideology of the regime, time and time again. I think that still holds true.

I do believe that the events of last year called the engagement paradigm into question, in the sense that it deepened the mistrust that any negotiating partner would have to feel in dealing with the Islamic Republic. This is a regime that could not treat its population, broadly, in a civilized fashion. So I think that it was appropriate that there was, in effect, a pause in the pursuit of engagement, but I do think that one has to approach the negotiating front with a priority on the issue at stake, which is the nuclear program. To ignore that, to push it off simply because of the reprehensible quality of many of the Iranian negotiating partners, is to lead us to even worse solutions ultimately down the line.

Question: I have a question primarily for Ambassador Djerejian. There are a bunch of states next to the Middle East who are allies of America called the European Union. What is your view of what their contribution should be and how America during the next two years could persuade them to do it?

Edward P. Djerejian: I think the Europeans have acted very constructively, especially in the Israeli–Palestinian context, and more so—the Europeans don't like to hear this— but with economic development aid and assistance, and technical aid, and political support for the negotiations when they were ongoing. So I think they can continue to play an important role.

But let me be candid here. I think at the end of the day, it is really going to be the United States that has to be the major interlocutor between the Israelis and the Palestinians, and, by the way, between Israel and Syria.

Question: I have another question about Iran. Is there a clear-cut [Barack H.] Obama administration policy with regard to Iran becoming nuclear? Is it that we will do everything short of war, with the phrase "all options are on the table," but really we mean we wouldn't go to war? You talked about positive momentum, but you also threw in that Iran is likely to renege on or renegotiate any deals that it makes. So if they are continuing to develop this [technology], is it clear for the U.S. administration that the end result could be a nuclear Iran?

Maloney: I in no way speak for the administration, so I'm parsing rhetoric the same as anyone else here. The administration has never said that it takes the military option off the table, and I don't think that any U.S. administration can or will make such a statement. It does seem to me that both the [George W.] Bush and Obama administrations have invested in diplomacy and in trying to find a way out, and I think that while one has to always look toward the long term—and there are elements of the U.S. government that do plan for the long term and worst-case scenarios—there is still a viable prospect of trying to head off an Iranian nuclear weapons capability. As long as that prospect exists, that should be the focus of our efforts. It is not to say that it is an easy one, but that inevitably has to be the focus of U.S. diplomacy.

David Makovsky: In terms of connecting the dots about Iran, it is clear that its support for the spoilers like Hamas and Hezbollah have made the peace process that much harder. We could engage in speculation and say, well, if they didn't have that capability, the moderates like [Palestinian President Mahmoud] Abbas and the like would be less fearful of the spoilers. The spoilers feel like they have the wind at their backs by having Iranian support. So while the nuclear issue is key, and it might be symbolic, there is also ongoing economic assistance. When I sat with President Abbas, he told me that Iran gave Hamas $500 million a year. Whether the figure is accurate I don't know, but that's what he says.

So they are posing a challenge for the United States on the nuclear issue, and they are posing a challenge by their support for these proxy groups. As Ed [Djerejian] pointed out, they have 40,000 rockets. A lot of those 40,000 rockets of Hezbollah are coming from Iran, some are coming from Syria. Some are Iranian rockets coming via Syria to Hezbollah.

[Question beyond the purview of the panel omitted.]

Question: The discussion on Israeli–Palestinian peace so far has not directly addressed the split in the Palestinian polity or the cultural, geographical, and economic split between the West Bank and Gaza. Do we have a realistic chance to achieve a two-state solution while those splits persist, and what are the range of policy options that we can and should consider to address it?

Makovsky: It's a very good question, a very legitimate question. I think here you get into some real issues. If you quietly speak to the senior reaches of the Palestinian Authority, they are not encouraging any sort of a dialogue with Hamas. They don't believe it will work. They believe that it will just cut the legs out from under them because if you could take Hamas' views and be a legitimate interlocutor, they would look like quislings. That's their view.

The second element here—and I'm saying what the Palestinians are saying to me—if we in Washington think that it's only about power for Hamas, and that you could just create all sorts of paradigms, that in fact they have these ideological attachments with the Muslim Brotherhood, and that's very real. I think we have been taking our cues, people think we take our cues from the Israelis, but I think we take our cues more from the Palestinian Authority on this.

I think right now, our approach should be a humanitarian one at this point. We should always have the arm outstretched if Hamas wants to do as the Quartet says, and those are the three conditions that the Quartet puts forward—it's not American conditions, Israeli conditions, it's the U.S., the European Union, Russia, and the UN [United Nations] on this.[1] Hold out hope.

The Israelis used to say that as long as they are divided, there's no use talking to them, and until Hamas rejoins the fold, we're not talking to the Palestinian Authority. They have come off that. It's crucial. I think Edward Djerejian and I see it very similarly. There is an urgency right now to really move forward on the Palestinian track, and I don't think it should be held hostage to the Gaza situation. But I think we have to

1 These two entities and two countries have become known as the Quartet, a loosely linked group that is seeking resolution of the issues outstanding with Iran.

make sure on a humanitarian level all is done, and we have to hold out the prospects that they could join in the future. But right now, let's not hold things up.

Djerejian: If I could put a plug in for something we did at the Baker Institute, we did a report—it took two years to write—it's called *Getting to the Territorial Endgame of an Israeli-Palestinian Peace Settlement*.[2] The only reason I'm referencing it is because we had credible Palestinians, credible Israelis, and we did a track II exercise. The endgame of that exercise was that in attacking—as [U.S. Special Envoy] George Mitchell has been doing—the territorial component of peace between the Israelis and the Palestinians, it is doable. We confronted all the major issues on the settlements, exchange of territory, common criteria, and we got the Israelis and the Palestinians to a point where there was a compromise solution on territorial swaps and exchange of territory, between 3.4 and 4.4 percent, which could accommodate most of the Israeli settlement blocks. We briefed Mitchell and the Obama team. We briefed [Israeli Prime Minister Benjamin] Netanyahu's national security team, and [Palestinian President] Abu Mazen personally.[3] The only point I'm making is that it can be done, despite all the obstacles.

Question: President Obama took a very [inaudible] initiative during the first year of his presidency, that he appointed Senator George Mitchell as the special envoy for the Middle East, which was something very rare. I would like to know, after this [midterm] election where Republicans have regained majority in the House of Representatives in a big way, how it will impact the initiative, and how it will impact the ability of President Obama's administration to be effective. What do you think, knowing the fate of negotiations in the past, the fate of dialogue in the past between the Palestinians and the Israelis, how optimistic or pessimistic, or what degree of guarded optimism do you have?

Makovsky: I think you're asking a very important question. I don't know if we know all the answers yet, coming right after the midterms. I just saw something from Richard Haass, and I agree with him, which is that the congressional dimension is best suited

---

2 *Getting to the Territorial Endgame of an Israeli-Palestinian Peace Settlement* (Houston, TX: James A. Baker III Institute for Public Policy, 2010; online at http://www.bakerinstitute.org/publications/BI-pub-IPTerritorialEndgame-020210.pdf).

3 Palestinian President Mahmoud Abbas is also widely known, particularly in the Arab world, by the kunya Abu Mazen.

to deal with budgets, appointments, and treaties.[4]

There are different schools [of thought] on how a Republican takeover of the House is going to impact U.S. policy. There are different views. Some say it will be a profound constraint because Obama will need the Republicans on other issues and they will be more difficult dealing with some of his initiatives. Others say they will so throttle his domestic initiatives that he will become a 100-percent foreign policy president.

I tend to think the third year of American presidential trajectories is one usually of activism. I tend to think he will not feel constrained, but we shall see.

But there is an area that I am very concerned about, and I alluded to very briefly in my remarks; I didn't want to dwell on it because of a lack of time, but no one has written about this yet. But I'm sure they will. That is the funding of the Palestinian Authority in the U.S. Congress. I think you had a few people who were passionately committed to it. A fellow by the name of Howard Berman [D-CA], who is the chairman of the House foreign relations committee. A woman by the name of Nita Lowey [D-NY], who is the head of what's called the Foreign Operations Committee—that is the foreign aid committee in the House.[5] Those are two people who really took this issue on. They also supported [U.S. Army Lieutenant] General [Keith W.] Dayton's effort to equip and train Palestinian security forces. They are up to over 3,000 people they have trained, and the security situation is fantastic on the ground, better than it has ever been in its history.

I'm worried that these programs are going to come under political pressure, that [Palestinian National Authority Prime Minister Salam] Fayyad—who everyone sees (the Israelis too) as very accountable, who is trying to create a culture of accountability and replace [Yasir] Arafat's culture of victimhood—that his ideas might not win the same resonance on the Republican side. They should, because the same ideas of accounta-

---

4 The reference is most likely to an interview with Richard N. Haass, president of the Council on Foreign Relations, that was posted online on the day before Makovsky was speaking: Council on Foreign Relations, "Obama's Political Obstacle Course," November 3, 2010, http://www.cfr.org/publication/23304/obamas_political_obstacle_course.html. See also an opinion piece that Haass published on November 18 titled "American Foreign Policy after the Mid-Term Elections," http://www.cfr.org/publication/23471/american_foreign_policy_after_the_midterm_elections.html.

5 Through 2010, Lowey chaired the House Appropriations Subcommittee on State and Foreign Operations.

bility and transparency are those that Republicans say they support. So I would hope if they got to know him, they would support him.

But what I wonder about is an across-the-board slashing of foreign aid—that is, not directed against the Palestinians, but is across the board—where they will be hurt. The program of the USSC [U.S. security coordinator], with the security effort of Dayton, and now [U.S. Air Force Lieutenant] General [Stephen P.] Muller, will be hurt. I think we should not let that happen. I think it's too important.

Djerejian: I think President Obama made a very wise decision when he came into office. He invested his presidency immediately on trying to resolve the Arab–Israeli conflict. He appointed George Mitchell at the outset. I think he took a page of lessons learned from both the George W. Bush and Bill Clinton administrations, where his two predecessors got engaged in Arab–Israeli conflict resolution, but very late in their mandates. That was smart. I think his political intuition is right on this one. I think his political instincts, his intellectual instincts, are right on this one. He wants to try to be the American president who can bring this together. I hope he will not be discouraged because of the elections, and that he will follow his political instincts and not listen to all the naysayers [about the] many reasons not to get engaged.

What do you aspire to political power and leadership for? What is your legacy? It is better to try, and I hope that he will persevere on trying to be the broker of an Israeli–Palestinian peace, and hopefully a more comprehensive agreement.

Joost Hiltermann: Speaking of special envoys, I just want to note the absence of a special envoy for Iraq. The task has been given essentially to Vice President Joe Biden, who has many other things on his plate. He has dealt with the Iraq file ably, I would say, but Iraq deserves more attention than it is getting. We are facing a year in which there ought to be a responsible exit strategy. So far, we have a deadline, we have an intent to withdraw, but really no strategy. I think it would require the efforts of a specially dedicated U.S. envoy to help navigate this very difficult process.

I would also say that special efforts would have to be directed toward one of the key fault lines in Iraq, the Arab–Kurdish one, centered on the question of Kirkuk. It will be very important for the United States to have a vision as to how to address this question before and after the withdrawal of American troops this year.

Question: The big problem in Afghanistan now is the Taliban and the support they are getting from Pakistan. The news reports that President Obama is heading on an Asia trip starting in India, where he going to give them, or arrange the sale of, a large number of C-130s and C-5s. It seems to me that that's the worst possible signal to send to Pakistan, who we want to cooperate with us in cracking down on the Taliban, just in terms of making them totally paranoid about Indian capabilities to project power into Afghanistan. Would you agree with my assessment?

Djerejian: Yes, the president is going to India; it's a very important relationship. But that's only part of the equation. Don't forget all the military aid and economic aid we're giving to Pakistan, and the strong support we are giving to that government. So the Pakistanis cannot consider this a zero-sum game. Pakistan is being very heavily supported by the United States politically, economically, and militarily.

Again, as I tried to say in my brief remarks, we have to connect the dots. We shouldn't segment our policy in bilateral prisms. It's not U.S.–India only, U.S.–Pakistan only. It's U.S. with South Asia, with the Kashmir issue as something we should nudge them along. They don't want us to, but we should be nudging them along on that, because Kashmir is the one issue that can bring these two nuclear powers to war, India and Pakistan. Therefore, I hope the president's trip to India will build up our credit in India so that he can use it in a more strategic framework on Afghanistan.

[Moderator notes that Afghanistan-Pakistan issues will be discussed in more depth by a later panel.]

Question: My question is to Suzanne [Maloney] and Ambassador Djerejian. Suzanne, you mentioned something about a lot of talk in Washington these days about a war [with Iran]. Ambassador, you also commented on the issue of sending an ambassador to Syria. These two issues really affect the majority of pro-freedom, pro-democracy Lebanese people. They feel there is a threat to the Lebanese state these days from an approaching war, and it looks like the administration has a lot of tactics and less strategy. So how would you address the Lebanese fear, and what should or could be done to avoid it?

Maloney: I will try to answer the Iran component of your question. Let me try to be more clear. I don't endorse the idea of military action toward Iran to deal with the nuclear issue, or to deal with a broader Iranian threat around the region, nor, frankly, do I think it's a likely outcome from this administration, even with more pressure from a Republican-dominated House. I think it's difficult to tamp down this talk in part because, as I said, no administration is ever going to take the prospect of military action off the table, nor should they. But it is much more an issue that gets bandied about by journalists, by think tanks, by people who, like us, have the luxury of engaging in the hypothetical.

The administration at this point, as far as their public statements are concerned, as far as everything that I think we can see in reading the tea leaves of what their actions are, is really gearing up for more diplomacy on Iran. Some of that diplomacy will incorporate negotiations, hopefully successful ones. Some of that diplomacy may incorporate more sanctions and more international pressure on Iran. I don't see an administration at this stage which is gearing up for war.

I think much of the media and punditry talk about the prospects, and even the likelihood, of war, either from the U.S. or from Israel toward Iran, is an overreaction to what happened with Iraq. While I understand that kind of an overreaction, I think it is unfortunate, because it skews the discourse and it eliminates the concern about what I see to be one of the more likely outcomes of our current policy course: a very long and frustrating increasing isolation of Iran, which does not produce a better outcome in the long term for any of the issues that we have on the agenda here today, or for Lebanon.

Djerejian: I really didn't understand your question on our ambassador in Syria. Was it a question or a comment?

Question: It's a question. The Lebanese pro-democracy and pro-freedom majority think the American approach is tactics more than strategy toward Syria, especially given that in the last two years, nothing really has been achieved, no improvement with the Syrian regime.

Djerejian: I'm an advocate of, again, connecting the dots. Lebanon's independence and evolution as an independent country cannot be achieved without bringing the Syrian equation into play. When I was ambassador to Syria in the 1990s, American policy was very instrumental in ending the civil war in Lebanon, with our other Arab allies. We were able to maintain our principled position on Lebanon, that no matter what the United States would do in terms of its relations with Syria—but also more importantly in terms of Israeli–Syrian peacemaking—it would not be done at the expense of Lebanon's political independence, sovereignty, and territorial integrity. When I was assistant secretary of state for the Middle East in the transition from Bush 41[6] to Bill Clinton, the first meeting we had with then-Prime Minister Rafiq Hariri that President Clinton had, President Clinton asked me, "What is the most important message I should convey to the prime minister of Lebanon?" I told him exactly that: "Mr. President, whatever we do on the Israeli–Syrian peace track will not be at the expense of our commitment to Lebanon's political independence, territorial integrity, and sovereignty."

My view is that we have to be totally represented in these capitals. We should be having a dialogue with Syria. An American dialogue with Syria would be very important

---

6 George H.W. Bush, the 41st president.

in terms of what happens in Lebanon also, to say nothing about the Israeli–Syrian relationship.

Barbara K. Bodine: Why don't we take one more speaker from each [microphone], each ask your question, and then I'm going to let every member on the panel wrap up your questions and make some final comments.

Question: My question is for Ms. Maloney. Do you think we should utilize Turkey in an attempt to help negotiate a solution with Iran? They seem to have positive relations with both the United States and Iran.

Question: My question is very clear and straightforward. Concerning the Israeli–Palestinian peace negotiation, wouldn't the concept of a Jewish state undermine these peace talks? Wouldn't it be considered as a new ethnic cleansing, considering the Palestinian who has Israeli citizenship inside Israel? What will happen to these Palestinians when we declare a Jewish state where the Israeli citizenship is only for Jewish people?

Makovsky: I guess I'll take the Jewish state question. If you look at the statements of the United States, statements of European leaders—Britain, France, Germany, even Russia—they have all said the idea of a Jewish state is something that is supported by all these countries. That was the whole idea of the UN partition plan; I think it was mentioned there 30 times. But the way they say it is to do it in a way that makes clear that it is with equal rights for all its citizens. That's something that Netanyahu has said at the Knesset just two weeks ago.

The other caveat would be that it does not prejudice any final status issues, meaning the refugee question, which is a legitimate topic for negotiation. So you could say you support the nation-state of the Jewish people with equal rights for all its citizens and without prejudice to any final status issue. That is part of America's commitment to the moral legitimacy of both a secure Israel and a just Palestine. I think that would work for all sides.

I think this is an issue that can be finessed. When you talk to Palestinians privately, they see it as a bargaining chip. They feel the Israelis have more chips than they do, and their view is they will play that card at the appropriate time. I hope there is a way to deal with that in a package approach so that each side feels that it gets something.

Hiltermann: I will take the first question and pretend you said Turkey's role vis-à-vis Iraq rather than Iran, leaving the Iran question for Suzanne. Turkey has been playing a very interesting role in the last few years as an emerging economic power in the region, developing free trade zones and very strong strategic relations with a number of countries in the region, including Syria and Iraq. There is some push back from fears of neo-Ottomanism, but by and large, Turkey's economic power also allows it to play a diplomatic role, which it very much would like to play.

That role could be very constructive. Again, I'll leave Iran aside for now. But in Iraq for sure, where Turkey has opened consulates in Basra, Mosul, and Irbil and has developed close relationships both with the Iraqi government and with the Kurdish regional government, it could play a very important mediating role between the two sides, between the central government and the Kurdish regional government, exactly on that fault line I mentioned earlier, the Kurdish–Arab one. Turkish nationalism is the third nationalism coming in there, after the Kurdish and the Arab one, and the Persians still on the sidelines of that. Because the Turkmens are such a small community, Turkey cannot really represent that community; it has to have wider interests, and it does. It also has significant energy interests in Iraq.

All of this makes for a very interesting combination. I think we need to look very closely at what Turkey will be doing in the coming years. I suspect it will be a fairly constructive role that will benefit the unity of Iraq.

Maloney: I'll speak quickly to the Turkey question and then maybe make one final wrap-up point. In terms of Turkey, I think the simple answer is "yes." We should try to use them as a potential mediator in dealing with the Iranian nuclear issue because clearly the Iranians have sought them out, and invested some energy in the relationship, and appear to trust them. And frankly, because the one time where we negotiated an enduring solution to a really tough issue—the Algiers Accords [1981], which concluded the hostage crisis—we relied on a third-party interlocutor [Algeria] to help both sides interpret the other because we just didn't understand the dynamics of the Iranian negotiators or the Iranian political situation. I think it was equally true on the other side, and those factors are present today.

I'd say it's not terribly likely in the short term that the Turks are going to emerge in a prominent role on the Iranian issue, simply because the administration really felt very badly served not just by the Tehran Declaration, the Turkish–Brazilian attempt to mediate last spring, but also by the Turkish decision to cast a "no" vote at the UN Security Council on sanctions. That left a great deal of bitterness that has played out somewhat in public, but I suspect remains in private [as well].

One final wrap-up comment on the domestic political environment here, which I didn't address when it came up in the question. I do think, as I said in my talk, that there is at least a prospect on the horizon of a modest agreement with the Iranians, some version of the TRR [Tehran Research Reactor agreement] that has been bandied about for the past year. The danger in this political environment is that it will be immediately attacked by the Republicans as a nonanswer to a very urgent problem, something that we all know it to be. But if indeed such an agreement can be concluded, if we can come to some agreement with the Iranians—to have a confidence-building measure, even one that is imperfect, even one that doesn't begin to deal with the crux of the issue—to see a concession from the Iranians on the nuclear issue at this moment would be such an important achievement that we have to do our best to insulate it from the domestic political fray here in the U.S.

Djerejian: Very briefly, my hope is that President Obama, as he now goes into this phase of his presidency, will use the power of the presidency, and the White House, and the bully pulpit, to really try to obtain bipartisan support, given the elections we have just had in this country, on some of the key foreign policy challenges we face, be it with China, Russia, and what we have been discussing in the Middle East, especially on the Arab–Israeli conflict, how we deal with Iran, the endgame in Iraq, how we deal with Afghanistan, Pakistan, and India. To me, these are issues that should obtain bipartisan support. What I worry about is that if the more hardened views come into play, we will begin to shoot ourselves in our collective feet, and not be able to use all the tools of our diplomacy, and all of our power, to be able to pursue our national security interests that are so challenging, as we've discussed briefly on this panel. Again, just one minor example, but by not naming American ambassadors in critical posts, we are shooting ourselves in the feet. An American ambassador in a tough spot is not a political concession to your enemy.

A rally of newly sworn Hezbollah troops in Qana, Lebanon, on January 18, 2009.
(Corbis/EPA/Hassan Bahsoun)

PART TWO

NEW APPROACHES TO NON-STATE ARMED ACTORS

CHAPTER SIX

Negotiating with Terrorists

Mitchell B. Reiss

Terrorism trends indicate an arrow that points upward in the coming years. It is increasingly likely that the threats will increase. This statement is based on anecdotal evidence, the analysis by counter-terrorism experts, and governmental reports and studies.

There will be more terrorist groups. They will have more places to gather and scheme, in the so-called "stateless zones," according to the CIA [Central Intelligence Agency] terminology. They will have access to more lethal weaponry.

There is also a demographic youth bulge across the Middle East that is likely to feed into some of the existing pathologies there. More than 60 percent of the people of this region are under the age of 25. It is likely that at least some of these—if it is only a small minority, it really doesn't matter—but some of these young men in particular will be attracted to militant extremism.

So the policy question, from an American perspective at least, is can we kill or capture all of these terrorists? The answer, of course, is probably not. Then that leads very quickly to another question: can we talk with some of them who may have local or more limited grievances? There is some supportive data out there, by RAND and by

Audrey Cronin and others, that 40 percent of all terrorist groups end by renouncing violence and joining a political process—four out of ten.[1] From the field, we hear from General [David H.] Petraeus, who is very fond of repeatedly saying we can't kill or capture our way out of industrial-strength insurgencies. So that means we may have to talk.

Is that a new approach to dealing with armed nonstate actors? Well, not really. It is as old as the founding of our country. Three of our Founding Fathers, our first three presidents, actually cut deals with the Barbary pirates. We passed legislation in Congress to pay them $2 million a year in tribute so they would not attack our merchant ships. But it certainly is a controversial policy, especially in the United States, to talk with these groups, to "negotiate with evil."

There are also many associated questions. When do you do that? Who do you talk to? How do you structure a conversation with these people? Do you fight and talk at the same time? That is not just an issue for governments; that is also an issue for terrorist groups. Do they decide to maintain the armed struggle while they are sitting down with government officials?

Do you structure the talks in secret? Almost invariably, governments do this, but then there is a moment when the talks need to come out of the shadows and into the light. The former head of MI5, Baroness Eliza Manningham-Buller, has said that is the most dangerous moment for governments. When you transition from secret to public talks, you lose control of a lot of these negotiations; you are being held hostage to other members of the terrorist group who may not be so enthusiastic, or may not even know that the leadership was talking to the government. You also have domestic constituencies, including the security and police forces, who may be less enthusiastic about it. Of course you have the families of the victims, which is always a very emotional pull on the heartstrings, especially when magnified by the media.

---

1 See Ben Connable and Martin C. Libicki, *How Insurgencies End* (Santa Monica, CA: RAND, 2010; online at http://www.rand.org/pubs/monographs/2010/RAND_MG965.pdf); Angel Rabasa, Stacie L. Pettyjohn, Jeremy J. Ghez, and Christopher Boucek, *Deradicalizing Islamist Extremists* (Santa Monica, CA: RAND, 2010; online at http://www.rand.org/pubs/monographs/2010/RAND_MG1053.pdf); Audrey Kurth Cronin, *How Terrorism Ends: Understanding the Decline and Demise of Terrorist Campaigns* (Princeton, NJ: Princeton University Press, 2009).

Then there is another question: Is the person you are talking to a reliable partner? Terrorist groups are not monolithic. They have different views and opinions. Is the person you're talking to the "right" person?

There are few good answers to these questions. When I posed them when I was serving at the State Department a few years ago, I wasn't able to get a whole lot of very good answers to these and other questions as I was starting to embark on my job as special envoy to the Northern Ireland peace process. A search of the open literature also didn't help me very much. We know that there has been an awful lot of government experience over the years having these types of engagements, but most of them have been in the shadows; very few have been memorialized. The information and the knowledge hasn't been captured—until now, and here's where I shill my book. It is called *Negotiating with Evil: When to Talk to Terrorists.*[2] It is the product of the past three years of my traveling around the world talking to counterterrorism experts, government ministers, military officials, negotiators, and former terrorists to try to see if we could get some lessons from the experiences that clearly are out there, so that government policy makers will have a little bit of guidance going forward when they ask themselves these same questions.

I looked at four states that governments engaged: the UK [United Kingdom] and the IRA [Irish Republican Army]; Spain and the Basque terrorist group ETA [Euskadi Ta Askatasuna]; Sri Lanka and the Tamil Tigers; and the U.S. military and the Sunni tribes [in Iraq]. Then I looked at one government that has decided not to engage with a group it labels terrorist: Israel and Hamas. Actually, as many of you know, that relationship between Israel and Hamas is much more complicated than simply a blanket policy of never negotiate.

There were a wealth of lessons from each of these case studies, and there were many more questions that came up. But I did think that there were some transcendent les-

---

2 Mitchell B. Reiss, *Negotiating with Evil: When to Talk to Terrorists* (New York: Open Road Integrated Media, 2010 [e-book only]).

sons that might be useful to share that also will be applicable more broadly across the Middle East and elsewhere. I want to talk about four very briefly.

The first is that a negotiation with these groups is "war by other means." You either have to defeat them militarily on the battlefield, wherever that might be, or you have to demonstrate the resolve at least not to lose for as long as it takes. You have to eliminate hope that they can fight their way, bomb their way, terrorize their way to victory. In the UK, that took 15 to 20 years. It was only in the mid-1980s that the IRA leadership started rethinking its approach. I had a revealing conversation with [Sinn Féin president] Gerry Adams about this in which he told me, when we were focusing on exactly this period, "Dialogue is essential. The alternative is war forever. We were not prepared to do that." Until you have that mind-set, you're not going to be able to get any farther with any of these negotiations.

I also saw in the research on the Tamil Tigers that [Velupillai] Prabhakaran, the leader of the Tamil Tigers, would call timeouts periodically when he was under financial strain or military strain from the government. We saw this even in the case of Hamas and Sheikh [Ahmed] Yassin. If you look at the timing of the *hudna* [truce] that he suggested to the Israelis, it was after a particularly intense military, financial, and political campaign by Israel to go after Hamas's senior leadership that these would bubble up.

The second lesson is the role of intelligence. That sounds obvious; you have to have a first-rate intelligence service or else you are out of luck. But what surprised me most about the research was that governments are very slow to mobilize their resources to adequately deal with these types of threats. Often they don't have the language skills. More frequently—and this was a surprise—they don't have the legislation domestically in order to get themselves organized. There are bureaucratic overlaps and rivalries. It took the Brits about 15 years, and it was only during [Prime Minister Margaret H.] Thatcher's watch that this got fixed. One MI5 official called it a dog's breakfast of rival security entities that were playing in Northern Ireland. She sent a retired head of

MI6, Maurice Oldfield, up there to rationalize it and get it fixed, but it took a while.

In Spain after [Francisco] Franco, they didn't have the domestic legislation in place, so they did something that is tempting for many governments: they went off book. They used extrajudicial means. They formed a group called GAL [Grupos Antiterroristas de Liberación] that engaged in illegal assassinations of about three dozen suspected ETA members in both Spain and France.

With the United States in Iraq, initially, the emphasis of our intelligence community was on finding the WMD [weapons of mass destruction]. We had 1,400 personnel in Iraq in 2003 focused primarily on finding the WMD, not on talking to insurgents or understanding what the grievances were. I think we paid a price for that. We also had a lack of linguists as well.

The third lesson is that you need a partner for peace. What a great euphemism: we need a partner for peace. We hear it all the time. In fact, that's not quite right. You need a particular type of partner, one that is exceedingly rare to find, somebody with the skill sets that are needed. They have to have credibility among their comrades. Often that person will have "blood on his hands" in order to demonstrate to the other hard men that he's got credibility. That person also has to have the imagination to envision a different way forward for the organization. He has to have physical and moral courage, and he also has to have the charisma and leadership to be able to bring his group out of the jungle, out of the mountains, out of the streets, and into a political process that eventually will result in peace, or at least conflict mediation.

I thought of calling the book, instead of *Negotiating with Evil, In Search of Gerry Adams*. As you look around the world, there are very few terrorist groups that have that charismatic leadership, that imagination, that physical and moral courage that Adams demonstrated in Northern Ireland. If you don't have that, you are not going to get very far in the negotiation.

The United States was extremely fortunate in Iraq, in Anbar Province, in finding—by happenstance, as it turns out—a young tribal elder called Abdul Sattar Abu Risha. He was found by accident. It wasn't clear that he was the man who was going to lead the Anbar Awakening. He came from a fairly disreputable tribe. There are some wonderful stories in the book about how the other Sunni sheikhs viewed Abu Risha. Again, without somebody like that, we were really going to be in even worse shape than we were at the time.

The fourth lesson I want to leave you with is patience. Patience isn't just a virtue, it's a strategic advantage. Governments have to realize when they engage with these groups that it is not just going to take months or years. It may take decades. You have to understand that going in. It is always going to take longer to negotiate with these groups than you anticipate. For one thing, terrorist groups aren't terribly sophisticated. You have to educate them, you have to coach them up. You have to explain to them some of the other things that they may not be aware of, since they have been hunkered down either in the jungle or the mountains for many years. They need to be able to understand your perspective and your constraints as well. This happened with the Sri Lankans. The Tamil Tiger negotiators weren't very good and really hampered the government over the years.

To go back to the IRA, their first meeting with the Brits in 1972 was almost like an episode of *Keystone Kops*, [with] lots of amateur mistakes, things that they wanted the Brits to do that were almost laughable in retrospect. I laid these out to [former IRA leader] Martin McGuinness last year and said, how could you guys do this? Martin told me, "I was only 22 at the time." That's exactly right. Nobody in the IRA had engaged in this type of negotiation for over 50 years, since Michael Collins. Martin is a very smart guy, and he's a very good public official today,[3] but he was only 22. The other guys were in their early twenties as well. They had no experience. So you have to be very patient.

---

3 At the time of publication, McGuinness is a member of Parliament of the United Kingdom of Great Britain and Northern Ireland and is deputy first minister of Northern Ireland.

What goes along with that is that these groups have very shallow talent pools. There aren't a lot of people who can actually represent the group. In addition to that one leader, they don't have a very deep bench. So the idea that you are going to put a grand bargain on the table and hope that you can tie up all the loose ends—security, diplomatic, economic, reconstitution, transition, integration—the idea that you're going to do that all at once is laughable. They can't. They are just not built for that. They don't have that ability.

These are some of the lessons that I have learned over the last three years. I think some of them are applicable. Hopefully, they will provide some guidance to policy makers going forward, and hopefully, they will be able to help us bring peace and justice to some of these conflicts around the world.

CHAPTER SEVEN

State versus Nonstate Inter-Ventions in Fragile States

David Kilcullen

I run a little company called Caerus Associates. We spend a lot of time working in fragile states around the world. We work on a lot of alternative energy, peace building, and community-based development work. What I want to do in this presentation is share some tentative observations from our current work on the issue of state versus nonstate interventions in fragile states. I am fairly liberally interpreting the panel topic of new thinking about nonstate armed groups.

When the international community intervenes in complex emergencies in fragile states, the response tends to have four key characteristics that you see repeated again and again, whether you are talking about nation-states intervening or international organizations intervening. First, it tends to be state-based. It tends to focus on government. It tends to be top-down. It focuses on the central government. It tends to be very focused on institutions, creating effective ones, or at least shoring up existing institutions of some kind—a central government structure. And it tends to be security-oriented, which tends to make it exclusive. We tend to go into an environment with the agenda of building institutions of a central state which the international community can recognize. People who have a different agenda tend to be classified as "enemy." They tend to be excluded from the process. So we often find ourselves engaging in conflict.

But what we have found in our work, and what I previously found in field research over about 20 years or so, with insurgents and terrorist groups mainly in the Middle

East and Southeast Asia, is that in conditions of state collapse, fragility, and complex emergencies, political authority actually tends to ebb away from the very institutions that the international community is trying to set up. Political power flows from central to regional and then to local groups. It flows away from civilian leaders to people with weapons. And it flows away from the formal institutions of the state to informal setups and institutions at the community level.

The international community prefers to work with centralized authority—state institutions led by civilian or at least nonarmed actors. The reality in these environments tends to be that political power has diffused to the local level, to community-based armed groups. That creates a conundrum. We come in with an approach that is very well suited to stable environments and very well reflects international norms, but it is badly suited to the actual power realities of the environments where we intervene, where the real power and the ability to resolve conflict or the ability to perpetuate violence seemingly endlessly does not actually lie with the people we are engaging with, but rather with nonstate local community groups, rather than the institutions of a central state. The result is often more chaos and even more violence over time.

Let me give you three examples. The first is Iraq. Ambassador [Mitchell B.] Reiss just spoke very accurately about what happened in Anbar [Province] during the Awakening, but if you go back in the period of our intervention in Iraq to 2003, there was an extremely awkward period where military commanders, civilian officials, and a variety of other people wanted to engage with the very same tribes that put the Awakening together several years later. They wanted to engage with the same community groups that even then were already turning against al-Qaeda and some of the radical groups. But they were specifically banned from doing that by the Coalition Provisional Authority [CPA] under Ambassador [L. Paul] Bremer. CPA policy was not to engage with nonstate actors, not to engage with community leaders, and not to work with the tribes. In fact, the Awakening in Anbar was the fifth awakening, the fifth attempt by the tribes to turn against al-Qaeda. On the previous four attempts, we let them hang, and they were slaughtered, because our policy was not to work with nonstate groups.

In Afghanistan since 2001, we have seen a very similar situation. The international community, through the Bonn process, centralized political authority in the hands of somebody—President Hamid Karzai—who was too weak to exercise that authority on his own. So he had to make a series of deals with important players and actors within the Afghan political structure, which led to the fact that, on the one hand, we've got an Afghan government which on paper is the most centralized in the world, but on the other hand doesn't do much actual governing, because it can't.

One particularly good illustration of why this is a problem is in the rule-of-law sector. We went in, rewrote the Afghans' legal code for them, built a supreme court building in Kabul, started training judges and prosecutors, and [began] building from the top down a state institution of courts, prosecutors, and so on. The Taliban came in at the local level with mobile courts several months after we arrived and ate our lunch at the local level. They are now effectively administering rule of law across large parts of the south and east of the country through informal, community-based processes, while the institutions of the central state have yet to catch up.

But I think the classic example is neither Iraq nor Afghanistan, but actually Somalia. You may remember that in 1992 after the collapse of the [Mohamed] Siad Barre regime and the famine, the international community intervened in Somalia with a classic top-down, state-focused, international community-led effort. You know, "You little natives get out of the way while us white guys tell you how this is going to be. We're going to back up the big democracy truck, unpack progress, and everything is going to be fine." The result has been a near-total failure.

In the north of the country during the same time frame, the same ethnic groups following the same state collapse, the same famine, and the same civil war went ahead and did things their own way with a bottom-up process that wasn't a process of security enforcement; it was a process of peace building. The clans got together in 1992–93 and made local-level peace deals. In 1993–94, those local-level peace deals resulted in regional charters. By the end of 1994, there was a provisional government in place, acting not only without the support of the international community, but in fact against active opposition from the international community, including the United Nations at times. This year, they went through their third peaceful presidential transition of power. They have a functioning court system, police, a functioning economy, and trade unions. All the institutions have emerged that one might expect, but they emerged bottom-up from the community rather than being imposed top-down by international actors.

That is only one of a number of examples where we have seen a much better outcome result from bottom-up, community-based peace building rather than top-down security operations by the international community. I think that has led to some new thinking in the way we deal with these groups. The Sons of Iraq, the Sahwa, the Awakening during the surge in Iraq, was just one example whereby creating a partnership with local communities could transform a security environment, not by imposing security but by building peace, which then led to security.

In Afghanistan, there is a program called the village stability operation, sometimes known as the village security operation, which has been mischaracterized as a local police program. It is actually a community-based governance program where local community *shuras* (councils) get together and work on issues having to do with securing and feeding and sustaining their own local area. It works very closely with the community development council model, which is again not a state-based model and not focused on an exclusive security process, but focused on bottom-up peace building.

Going back to Africa briefly, the Office of Transitional Initiatives [OTI], which is one of USAID's most important innovations over the last 20 years—invented in 1994 to deal with the situation in the Balkans—has been extremely important in what we have done in Afghanistan and Iraq. But I want to take you to one example of the sorts of interventions that we can do that may be a little more effective than turning up with 20,000 Marines and trying to solve the security problem.

In late July 2005, there was a helicopter crash in southern Sudan. A helicopter belonging to President [Yoweri K.] Museveni of Uganda crashed and killed, as part of the crash, the vice president of independent south Sudan, John Garang. That incident resulted in three days of major rioting across Sudan. At least 150 people were killed, more than 2,000 people were arrested. There was a large amount of communal violence across the south and center of the country. A peace deal which had just been put in place to resolve 21 years of civil war was very much in jeopardy. It was a situation somewhat analogous to the airline crash in Rwanda that led to major conflict in 1994.

How was that major conflict averted in the case of Sudan? It was averted because John Garang's widow [Rebecca Garang] got onto a radio and broadcast to the community of southern Sudan: "Hey guys, this was an accident, relax." The community calmed down, a lot of the violence went away. How did John Garang's widow get onto a radio? Because OTI had put in an extremely limited, small-footprint, carefully targeted intervention of creating local-level radio stations so that people could communicate with each other across southern Sudan. No big institutions, no troops, no large aid programs, just a mechanism which allowed people who were already making peace among themselves to communicate that peace process to each other. That very small-scale, largely unknown aid intervention in southern Sudan averted in July–August 2005 a similar situation to what may have happened in Rwanda.

So limited, targeted intervention that focuses on enabling civil society to solve its own problems seems to be something that works better than the traditional international community intervention. That is just what we are seeing in the field right now. It is changing some of the ways that we do business. I think what we are starting to see is new thinking about posture, about how to create the right posture to allow local civil society to fulfill that function of local-level peace building, about what is the right military posture, the right governance posture, the right trade posture, the right foreign assistance posture, and so on, to enable civil society to engage in bottom-up, community-led peace building that is inclusive rather than exclusive.

There is a military role in that. Some of the people in these environments will not negotiate and just need to be taken out of the picture. That's OK, but it's a very limited, carefully targeted role, just like all the other aspects of international community intervention.

On the whole, I think we are coming to the view, which may perhaps be entirely obvious to people in this room but hasn't always been policy in places like the World Bank or NATO or the U.S. government, that we need to be adopting the least intrusive, least expensive approach focusing on processes rather than structures, focusing on communities and not just on governments, and trying to be inclusive rather than exclusive.

CHAPTER EIGHT

WHAT ARE OUR OBJECTIVES WITH NONSTATE ACTORS?

ROBERT MALLEY

When we are talking about armed nonstate actors—and in the region of the world that I work on, the focus is really on Hamas and Hezbollah—the question that people always ask, and the issue about which people get very quickly polarized (and I have been caught up in that debate) is, shall we talk to them or not? Should the United States talk to Hamas and Hezbollah?

I want to put that question to the side. I think that question has done more to pollute the debate, to divert attention from what the real issues are, than it has been a productive line of inquiry. That should be the end point—what we should do, whether we should talk to them. The first question should be to analyze where they come from, to analyze whether our policies so far have been successful in dealing with them and achieving our own self-proclaimed objectives, and if not, then let's look at alternatives.

I think there has been a confusion of means and ends and a rush to judge the means—should we talk to them—rather than the ends: what are our objectives when it comes to these nonstate armed actors? Again, I will focus mainly on those two because they have become so much of a part of the political debate here.

The first question is whether, measured by the United States's own self-proclaimed yardstick, our policies toward Hamas and Hezbollah have been successful. What have been the objectives? The objectives have been to weaken those movements. When it comes to Hamas in Gaza, the objective has been in some cases to defeat them militarily. The objective has been to get them to change their ideological posture, to accept the Quartet[1] conditions. When it comes to Hezbollah in Lebanon, the objective has been to disarm them.

On one issue after another—I don't think we really need to go down the list—but on virtually all of these standards, all of these measurements, I think the conclusion is relatively noncontroversial: we have not succeeded. Hamas may be less popular today, but it is firmly entrenched in Gaza. It has not accepted, and is not closer to accepting, the Quartet conditions. It acts as a constant factor in the negotiations, making it harder to reach an agreement, and making it harder for President [Mahmoud] Abbas to move forward, knowing that he has a powerful constituency that has powerful resonance among Palestinians, and Arabs more generally, and is looking and stirring behind his back. Hezbollah is no closer to being disarmed; in fact, it is probably more powerful today than it has ever been in its history, not just in terms of its weapons, but in its ability to paralyze the political process and the institutions in Lebanon. On issue after issue, whether it was the goal of making them change their worldview, whether it is the goal of weakening their hold in Gaza or their power in Lebanon, whether it is the goal of strengthening their opponents—Fatah in the Palestinian case, or March 14 Alliance in Lebanon—it is very hard to see in what way the policy has been successful.

That is the starting point for me. The starting point shouldn't be should we talk to them, in which case all these other issues come up. The starting point should be whether so far—again, judged by what the [George W.] Bush administration and now to some extent the [Barack H.] Obama administration have stated as their objectives— whether the policy of isolation, marginalization, attempts to disarm, or attempts to dislodge have been successful. I think the answer is pretty clearly "no."

So let's take that as a starting point. Now let me offer a series of observations about these two movements, but even more broadly, about nonstate armed actors in the

---

1 The Quartet on the Middle East, often referred to simply as the Quartet, includes the United States, the United Nations, the European Union, and Russia.

Middle East, to try to reach a conclusion about what might be alternative approaches to them.

The first observation is the fact that these movements over the past decade have become much more powerful, much more influential. Armed nonstate actors are nothing new to the Middle East. For those who have followed the history of Lebanon, this really looks like an old story. But there is something new about them because in the old days, they were far more extensions of—proxies of—established states and established regimes. What seems to have changed is that these have become much more holistic. They have much deeper national roots. They are acting often in conjunction with other states, but not on behalf of other states, and they have a much greater ability to appeal to their own local constituencies, not simply through the military option they offer, but through the social services that they provide, through charitable institutions, through a more holistic approach to their links to society. That is a change that is a function in part of the decreasing power of the central state, about which we just heard something, and their ability to make up for the deficiencies of that central state. So that is observation number one, an increase in power, but also a change in their role in their domestic societies and their ability to act independently of others.

The second observation is that these cases, Hamas and Hezbollah, but also to some extent the Sadrist movement in Iraq (another case that we have studied at the International Crisis Group),[2] all three movements have prospered precisely in societies that have an open wound, an unresolved question that polarizes domestic constituencies in those countries. Either questions about the nature of society—that's certainly the case in Lebanon and is the case in Iraq as well—or a question of their relationship with a third party, also the case of Lebanon vis-à-vis Israel and Lebanon vis-à-vis Syria, the case of the Palestinians vis-à-vis Israel. With all these cases, you have an unresolved, unaddressed, existential issue which divides the polity and in which the nonstate actor takes one side against the others.

2 See "Iraq's Muqtada al-Sadr: Spoiler or Stabiliser?" International Crisis Group, Middle East Report No. 55, July 11, 2006, http://www.crisisgroup.org/~/media/Files/Middle%20East%20North%20Africa/ Iraq%20Syria%20Lebanon/Iraq/55_iraq_s_muqtada_al_sadr_spoiler_or_stabiliser.ashx; "Iraq's Civil War, the Sadrists and the Surge," International Crisis Group, Middle East Report No. 72, February 7, 2008, http://www.crisisgroup.org/~/media/Files/Middle%20East%20North%20Africa/Iraq%20Syria%20Lebanon/ Iraq/72_iraq_s_civil_war_the_sadrists_and_the_surge.ashx.

These are also cases—and all three have this in common as well—where a certain constituency, if not all people in those entities, feel a security threat that the state is not able to address. Again, this was certainly the case in Lebanon. The experience of the Shi'ite community at the hands of Israel is one that is very profoundly entrenched in the psyche of Shi'ites and other Lebanese as well. It certainly was the case in Iraq, and it is the case in Palestine as well, where the Palestinian Authority, for all its achievements in some areas, has been singularly inept at protecting Palestinians from Israel. That of course feeds and fuels the desire and aspiration to have an organization that can defend and provide the kind of defenses that the central authority—or in the case of the Palestinians, the nonstate authority—can provide.

The third observation, which is also a common trait of these three cases, is that these are the cases in which the U.S. has invested most heavily, particularly after 2000, to shape the polity, to in some cases accelerate the holding of elections, and has been generally most invested. That certainly is the case with Iraq, with the invasion. It was the case in Lebanon after 2005, where the U.S. very powerfully tried to go in and take sides in domestic struggles and take sides with one against the other, and try to shape Lebanon in a certain way. It's the case in Palestine to this day, really triggered by the elections in 2006, elections which the United States had been promoting. But again, in all these cases, it is interesting to see that where the U.S. has been deeply involved in trying to structure and shape society and the polity in a certain way, these nonstate armed actors have prospered and flourished, in part by playing off against this polarization of us against them. Of course in their case, the "us" is very different from the "us" that President Bush had in mind.

The fourth observation, which is in many ways a consequence of what I just said, and the deep-rootedness of these movements in their own societies: military means to defeat them have not worked. It didn't work in the case of Hamas, whether it was Fatah and the Palestinian Authority that was going after it in Gaza or in Israel's war of

2008. It certainly hasn't worked in Lebanon, either, the war of 2006. In all of these cases, military means at best haven't worked, at worst have backfired, and in some cases have strengthened the hold of the entities that these military operations were designed to defeat.

The fifth observation is that one of the tools that the U.S. and others have used to try to diminish the influence and the resonance of these movements is by providing assistance to their opponents. A lot of the assistance has gone to the Palestinian Authority, to President Abbas, and support has gone to March 14. To a large extent, I think that misses the point. To say it quite crudely, President Abbas suffers from many things and faces many problems. One problem he doesn't face in the eyes of his own people is a perception that he is insufficiently supported by the United States. That is not why many Palestinians are questioning the legitimacy of the leadership, and there are a whole host of questions. But the notion that by giving more assistance to President Abbas somehow we can neutralize the perception that the current Palestinian leadership is too indebted to the West and not autonomous enough in its decision making seems, to me, misguided. So in a way, the more the U.S. pumps aid into the hands of those whom these movements are opposing, it validates—it may help them in some ways, but it also validates the narrative that Hezbollah and Hamas and others want to propagate, that the ones they are fighting are stooges of the West. So I think it's really a double-edged sword to keep in mind.

The sixth and final observation is that these movements feed on the underlying grievances that I mentioned earlier, these unresolved, core existential issues, and at the same time these issues can't be resolved if they are excluded. Just to take the two cases of the Palestinians and the Lebanese—and there may be disagreement on this—but my strong conviction is that it is going to be very difficult, if not impossible, to truly resolve the Israeli–Palestinian conflict if we don't address the question of Hamas, for all kinds of reasons having to do with the fact that they control Gaza; the fact that the

Palestinian movement is divided to an extent that I don't think any liberation movement has been divided and been able to reach an agreement by negotiating with its foe; and the legitimacy question that is hanging over the leadership in Ramallah. For all these questions, it reduces President Abbas's maneuvering room, and it makes it more possible for spoilers to step into the fray.

So the notion that you can move the peace process without addressing the question of Hamas seems to me to be an illusion. That is why the logic that I hear—which David Makovsky put forward earlier and which you hear all the time—let's move the peace process first, and then we'll find a way, Hamas will be confronting the dilemma of whether to join a process that's popular or oppose it—I don't think you will ever get there. Hamas has many tools and has shown time and again that it has the tools to sabotage, prevent, and simply to spoil a process from which it would be not just absent but of which it would be a target.

The same of course goes in Lebanon. The notion that one could have a stable government in Lebanon by excluding the most powerful representative of the most numerous constituency in Lebanon seems to me to be profoundly misguided. I think we have seen it. I think the Lebanese have paid the price for some of the illusions that the West had that they could build Lebanon by excluding a party that is not just a party, it is really the embodiment at this point of the Shi'ite constituency.

So for that reason, we are caught in this dilemma of how do you address these underlying grievances, which fuel the power of these movements, at the same time that you need to bring these movements, somehow, into the game if you want to be able to fully address those issues.

So we come to the question with which I began: what then? What are the options? What can we do if the policies of the past have failed and if we are confronting what is a major and significant factor, at least in those two contexts? Drawing from what I just said, I think the first rule is what not to do. The notion that you could marginalize, ignore, exclude, or try to defeat militarily, I think we need to put those options aside because they simply have not worked. We, the United States, don't have the means to accomplish them, and the people in the region cannot live with the consequences of our unsuccessfully trying to do so. It is just too costly for them.

I don't think the debate should be reduced to the question of whether we talk to them or not. I think Mitchell Reiss gave a presentation about different contexts where it may work or not. We talk to some, we don't talk to others. In some cases it may be premature, in some cases it may be futile, in some cases it may be counterproductive or too costly politically. We are in a very political city, and we know the cost sometimes of doing things. Even if they might be wise diplomatically, they may simply be too costly politically.

But it is a very reductionist view to believe that either you talk to them or you stay where we are today. There are a whole host of other instruments in our toolbox, from encouraging third parties to talk to them, but in an authorized channel, not the kind of talks that take place today—and of which I'm a part—where we talk to Hamas and Hezbollah and both sides get frustrated. Their side gets frustrated because we have nothing to offer, and we get frustrated because they are not giving us anything in return. So it becomes a bit of the dialogue of the dead. You need to think more about empowering third parties.

In the case of Hamas, it means not necessarily the U.S. talking to Hamas, but changing its attitude, its whole mind-set, when it comes to Palestinian reconciliation—to stop seeing it as an obstacle to peace, but rather as one of the preconditions for peace, which is to find a way to re-stitch the Palestinian national movement. It means changing our approach toward Gaza. It is not simply a humanitarian question, it is a political question. The humanitarian disaster in Gaza came about for political reasons, and it will be resolved when we reach a different political conclusion. It has to do with how we are prepared to deal with Hamas in Gaza.

In the case of Hezbollah, which I think is far more complex, far more complicated, for a whole host of reasons, I think it entails maybe not talking to Hezbollah—that may come later—but finding a different way to engage with Syria and at the very least not repeating the mistake of 2008, where the administration seemed, or at least March 14 in Lebanon seemed to believe that we would come to their assistance if they were in a confrontation with Hezbollah. As it turned out, they were left out there to dry, and we were not able to do anything to help them.

 | Rethinking A Middle East in Transition

In conclusion, there are two thoughts I want to leave with you. The first is that I think we have to escape the dual illusion that has too often handcuffed our policy: the belief that engagement is the ultimate reward that the United States can offer its foes, which is only the flip side of that other dangerous illusion, which is that isolation is a decisive penalty that we can inflict upon them. I think we need to escape both those ends of the spectrum.

One last thought. Mr. Reiss said something that I think is very important. Many of these movements don't have the experience, they don't have the wherewithal to really engage in the kind of talks we're talking about. They need training. I will just bring to your attention the fact that one of the things I think is extremely damaging: we have a law on the books here which prevents anyone not simply from giving money to terrorist groups, which I can understand, but from providing any form of material assistance, which the Supreme Court and the administrations have interpreted as including assistance in trying to train them in negotiations or train them in nonviolent means of resistance, or talk to them to give them advice about how to move from violence to nonviolence, or accepting the Quartet principles.[3] We are not allowed to do that. I think that is a profound irony, a profound disservice to the people in the region, and to ourselves.

3 See *Holder v. Humanitarian Law Project*, 130 S.Ct. 2705 (2010), http://www.supremecourt.gov/opinions/09pdf/08-1498.pdf.

CHAPTER NINE

De-radicalization and Disengagement Programs

Peter R. Neumann

This topic is one that has captured the imagination of policy makers from Riyadh to Washington, D.C., to the extent that some believe they have found the silver bullet in the fight against insurgents and terrorists, and that is de-radicalization and disengagement programs. For those of you who do not know what I am talking about, de-radicalization or disengagement programs are in essence rehabilitation programs. They happen usually in prisons. They target insurgents and terrorists who have been captured, trying to convince these people to abandon armed force. They help them reintegrate into society.

The International Centre for the Study of Radicalisation and Political Violence did a study on the effectiveness and the functioning of these programs.[1] We studied eight of them. Not all of our case studies were in the Middle East, but the majority were. There are some countries, such as Singapore and the Philippines, outside of the Middle East who are running these programs, but the majority of countries who are running programs are based in the Middle East. Our sample included arguably the most sophisticated program, the one in Saudi Arabia that many of you will have heard about, and arguably the least sophisticated and least successful program, the one that was running in Yemen until about five years ago. Here is an overview of what we found.

---

1 Peter R. Neumann, *Prisons and Terrorism: Radicalisation and De-radicalisation in 15 Countries* (London: International Centre for the Study of Radicalisation and Political Violence, 2010; online at http://icsr.info/publications/papers/1277699166PrisonsandTerrorismRadicalisationandDeradicalisationin15 Countries.pdf).

First, we looked at how these programs work. What are the core elements? What are the key underlying dynamics? In other words, if any of you wanted to construct a de-radicalization program, what kinds of things would you have to include in order to make it work? We believe that there are five ingredients, five key elements that are part of every successful and good de-radicalization program.

The first is a mix of different kinds of programming. You will have to have some sort of religious and ideological re-education, deconstructing key concepts that have been misunderstood, arguably, and reconstructing them in a more productive way in the minds of the participant. But typically, some of the good programs are combining the religious and ideological re-education with vocational training, offering the subjects not just a re-education about Islam, but also some of the skills that will provide them with the opportunity to make a living after they have been released.

The second ingredient is comprised of what we call credible interlocutors. These are people who look after prisoners throughout the duration of the program. They have to know their stuff, obviously. They need to be respected by the prisoners, either because of their religious knowledge or because, as in the case of the Philippines, for example, they are former insurgents themselves. In either case, what is really important about the people who are interacting with prisoners is that they have the ability to relate to these people. In Saudi Arabia, for example, even if you are an incredible authority on Islam, you will not be allowed to interact with prisoners unless you have proven your ability to establish what they call "brotherly relationships," to relate to people and their needs.

The third ingredient is that good programs are all focused on prisoners' transition from prison back into society. From day one, they will in essence start preparing prisoners for the day of their release, on the one hand by providing them with skills, but also, and importantly, by reestablishing the links to their families, which many of them had lost when it became obvious that they were engaged in armed violence. In fact, in the case of Saudi Arabia, for example, many of their families abandoned them. Family reconciliation, therefore, is incredibly important because it means on the day they will be released from prison, there is a positive influence waiting outside the prison walls, rather than a negative one.

That leads to the fourth ingredient, which is, more broadly speaking, that all good programs are about locking people into commitments. They are about increasing the social, material, and psychological costs of going back to insurgency. So it doesn't stop with family reconciliation, which is just one layer of commitment. Tribal reconciliation is almost as important. Saudi tribes will have to vouch for prisoners' good behavior. In Saudi, but also in other cases, prisoners are provided with jobs, apartments, cars, and in some cases they are provided with the ultimate commitment, namely a wife. All of this is about making sure that when they are released from prison, they have so much to lose that it would be almost irrational to go back to terrorism and insurgency. You would lose your family, your tribe would be against you, the security services would be chasing you once more, you would lose your wife, your apartment, your job, and your car. That is a lot to give up, and that is exactly the point of the program.

The final ingredient involves material incentives. I have mentioned some of these already. Material incentives are arguably the most controversial aspect of these programs because it looks like you are rewarding people for engaging in terrorism. Yet they are important, but they are not decisive on their own. In fact, all the programs which we have studied have relied to some extent on money and material incentives. But those that relied on money and material incentives alone were largely unsuccessful. Money and material incentives only work if they are part of that broader idea of creating commitments and locking people into obligations that they find hard to get out of. Money and material incentives are not likely to be successful if deployed on their own, as they were, more or less, in the Philippines.

So there you have it, five ingredients, a mix of programming, credible interlocutors, a focus on reintegration and aftercare, creating multiple commitments, and material incentives as part of a strategy to create commitment. So you can go off and do your own program now. Good luck.

Before you do so, however, I want to give you two warnings, which may also come back to the point of these programs being a silver bullet, which I believe they are not. The first point is that de-radicalization programs cannot really be studied in isolation of the conflicts in which they are being implemented. A lot of people are now studying these programs and trying to find metrics—in Washington, it's all about metrics all the time—as to what makes these programs successful. I think it is fatally flawed to look at these programs in isolation from the sort of social and political environment in which they are being implemented.

Take Iraq, for example. Most people believe that the program that was run in Iraq in 2007–8 was a big success. Undoubtedly—and David [Kilcullen] knows more about this than I do—perhaps it was. But I would also argue that the very same program that was run in Iraq in 2007–8—the exact same program, using the exact same measures—would have produced different outcomes had it been run in 2005. The reason is, of course, that the political situation in Iraq was completely different. In 2005, Iraq was on the brink of civil war, insurgency was gaining momentum, Sunni tribes were still opposed to the American presence. People would have been sent back into hostile communities. In 2007–8, the situation had been turned around and people were being sent back into communities that were actually supporting the effort that was going on as part of the program. So the exact same program implemented in the same country at a different point in time would have produced a different outcome. Political momentum plays an important role.

My final point relates to this one. It is quite clear that these programs, however good and sophisticated they are as programs, are not a solution in and by themselves. A de-radicalization program cannot solve a conflict, and it would be foolish to think so. Such programs are not a substitute for other means of conflict resolution. They always need to be embedded in a wider strategy. They need to be combined also with sometimes harder and perhaps more traditional counterterrorism and counterinsurgency measures. I am saying this not because I think you are naïve, but because I am hearing that a lot in my own continent in Europe and at the United Nations—people speaking about these programs as a substitute to some of the more traditional counterinsurgency measures. That is why in my own country, in Germany, people were so enthusiastic to give money for the emerging program in Afghanistan, because they see it as a substitute for sending more troops. But it is not. De-rad programs make a difference, but they rarely make a difference on their own. They have to be sophisticated and well-constructed, but they also need political momentum, and they need to be embedded in a wider strategy. Just having a program is necessary, but very rarely is it sufficient.

CHAPTER TEN

DISCUSSION OF NEW APPROACHES TO NONSTATE ARMED ACTORS

MODERATED BY ROGER HARDY

Question: I'd like to ask about something that has not been addressed yet: the criminalization of the nonstate actors. We have seen in a number of different settings—from Latin America with the FARC and Sendero Luminoso, in the case of Afghanistan with a whole plethora of the insurgency groups, including Taliban—an increasing reliance on participation in international drug trafficking, weapons trafficking, money laundering, and things like that. This is somewhat changing the character of the insurgencies. I'd like to hear perspectives on dealing with that dimension of this growing problem.

David Kilcullen: One of the things that can happen to an insurgency as it degrades—this happened in Northern Ireland, it certainly has happened in other insurgencies—is that it can turn into a criminal network. We also see examples such as Mexico, where some people were very quick to say that we're dealing with an insurgency, even though the motivations are primarily criminal and economic rather than political and ideological. So I think it's fairly clear in the field that there's an overlap between criminal behavior and the behavior of politically motivated groups like insurgents or terrorists.

Leaving aside the legal issues for a second, I think it's very important that we avoid criminalizing behavior unless we absolutely have to. Once you go down a certain path—for example, UN listing as a terrorist organization—a lot of the options that are open to you to deal with and resolve these problems go away. So there are times, obviously, when you're dealing with an out-and-out criminal group that is economically motivated, there are other times when you do need to criminalize behavior. But if you can avoid it, it's usually better, in my view.

Mitchell B. Reiss: I think you have the problem at both ends, actually. As David suggested, with a lot of these terrorist groups, they spill over into criminal activity to fund themselves. They are a hybrid at times. That certainly has been the case with many that we know of. But also from a governmental perspective, it is almost a philosophical question. Do they see this through a counterterrorism frame, or do they see it through a law enforcement frame? I think it's fair to say that the [George W.] Bush administration saw it more from a counterterrorism angle and the [Barack H.] Obama administration more from a law enforcement angle. That is going to create all sorts of consequences in terms of the tools that are available to you and some of the approaches that might be available.

What makes it difficult is that some of these terrorist groups are both. We haven't yet developed, in my opinion, a hybrid system from a governmental perspective as to how to deal with some of these threats out there. There has been talk about national security courts. There is a very good book by Benjamin Wittes at the Brookings Institution, I think the best book on the subject, calling for a hybrid approach.[1] So it's both the facts on the ground, but also from a governmental perspective what frame you view it, is going to have very important policy consequences.

Question: My question is the big, obvious question out there, with great implications for our policy makers. There is a lot of discussion about engaging with the Taliban. Since we have a panel of experts, what advice would you give to policy makers were they to pursue on that course? What obstacles should they expect, and how can they best achieve a solution?

Kilcullen: It depends on what you mean by Taliban, and it depends what you mean by engaging. There have been a lot of programs to engage with local-level fighters in

---

1 Benjamin Wittes, *Law and the Long War: The Future of Justice in the Age of Terror* (New York: Penguin Press, 2008).

Afghanistan, some of which have been quite successful. Most recently, about three weeks ago, 200 fighters reconciled with the government in Herat Province (they actually came from Helmand). There have been a number of other incidents throughout the summer of lower-level leaders and smaller groups putting their weapons down and rejoining the political process.

I've had conversations with tribal elders who have said to me that between 5 and 10 percent of the people we are fighting are committed ideologically in some way to the Quetta Shura, and that the other 90 to 95 percent are reconcilable under certain circumstances. I think that's very true, but I think that you have got to recognize that although the vast majority of successful counterinsurgencies end in a negotiated solution—something like 80 percent—you have to be negotiating from a position of strength. That's not where we are right now in Afghanistan at the moment, although we are getting there militarily.

The other issue is that there have been hundreds of deals struck with the Taliban over the years. Very few of those deals have lasted more than a few days or weeks. As Ambassador Reiss pointed out, having a viable interlocutor or a viable partner in negotiations is critically important. I'm not sure that we could put our finger precisely on who would be a reliable interlocutor for the Taliban right now. It's so disruptive a group, and so fragmented that any number of people could plausibly put themselves forward to negotiate. But it would be very difficult to believe that that negotiation would result in an outcome that would stick.

A final point would be that one of the things you can do when you target a terrorist group is not only disrupt it, but also shape it for negotiations; identify the people that are most willing to negotiate and deal with their rivals in order to strengthen the possibility of a peaceful outcome.

Roger Hardy: I'm going to give you guys a chance to come back on issues of your own choice. I'd like to keep the pace going a bit. Let's take three questions at a time and see if that works better.

Question: In addition to the various approaches you mentioned regarding nonstate armed groups, what about the disruptions of weapons and money to these groups? Based on your research, doesn't it make it easier, then, to bring them to the negotiating table? Specifically regarding Hezbollah, we see today that Hezbollah has lost in popularity. They have been losing elections, national elections, even lately the local elections. We have seen more challengers in their areas. Of course they have been isolated even by the Arab world, not just by the U.S. So if Hezbollah does not have the hundreds of millions of money coming out from Iran, and the weapons, wouldn't it make it easier for them to recognize the Lebanese legitimate institutions, to come to the negotiating tables, to be more willing to negotiate?

Question: My question is to Mr. Reiss. You mentioned that the success of General [David H.] Petraeus in Iraq was achieved after finding [Sheikh Abdul Sattar] Abu Risha, who unified the tribes against al-Qaeda. Do you think that if he doesn't find an Abu Risha in Afghanistan, then there will be no success?

Question: Mitchell Reiss mentioned that with the passage of time, there could be even more terrorists or militants. This war has been going on for the past full decade. Isn't it time that those people who are involved in mediating, educating them, bringing them to the mainstream, do they need to review their approach? With the passage of time, there is more resistance, the number is increasing. Nobody can claim when this thing will be brought to closure.

Robert Malley: I have several comments on your question on Hezbollah. I think clearly if the international community could stop the flow of money and weapons, it would weaken Hezbollah. That was the goal of [United Nations] Security Council Resolutions 1559 and 1701.[2] And look where we are. You won't be able to deal with

---

2 United Nations Security Council Resolution 1559, adopted on September 2, 2004, reiterated "strong support for the territorial integrity, sovereignty and political independence of Lebanon within its internationally recognized borders" (http://daccess-dds-ny.un.org/doc/UNDOC/GEN/N04/498/92/PDF/N0449892.pdf). United Nations Security Council Resolution 1701, adopted on August 11, 2006, called for "a full cessation of hostilities," particularly those instigated by Hezbollah, and reiterated support for the provisions of all previous resolutions, including 1559 (http://daccess-dds-ny.un.org/doc/UNDOC/GEN/N06/465/03/PDF/N0646503.pdf).

it if you can't address the question of Syria, which brings us back to the earlier panel and the whole question of the peace process. So yes, as an objective, but since 2006, if anything, the trends have been in the other direction.

You say Hezbollah has been weakened. We could debate the extent to which it has been weakened. I think the Shi'ite community, from my experience—and you may have more—has an ambivalent relationship. They are dissatisfied with parts of Hezbollah's performance, its ideology. They may not espouse its very close relationship to Iran. So it may have anger, may have frustration, may have some dissent, but it has no alternative. I think the Shi'ite community for now is very much united behind Hezbollah. Hezbollah hasn't been losing elections; it wins the elections in the Shi'ite community. The rest, yes, you are right, in the last elections, General [Michel N.] Aoun and others may not have done quite as well. But Hezbollah has no real rival for the loyalty of its constituency.

So I don't think we can expect them to be weakened in any significant way. One has to take a more comprehensive view. It does come back to the question of Syria. It ultimately comes back to the question of Iran, and those are bigger issues that the United States needs to tackle.

Reiss: Let me talk about Abdul Sattar [Abu Risha]. A couple years ago, David Rose wrote an article in *Vanity Fair* in which he said that the United States missed this wonderful opportunity to actually end the insurgency in 2004–5 because we refused to talk to a number of Anbari sheikhs who were camped out in Amman, Jordan.[3] They had been telling us that they could turn off the insurgency like a faucet, and if only we would support them, give them arms and money, all of our problems would go away. One of the things that the chapter [in my book] on the Anbar Awakening does is to investigate that pretty thoroughly and discredit that whole idea. Those guys did not possess the qualities that you need—for one thing, they were not even in the country—that Abdul Sattar had.

---

3 David Rose, "Heads in the Sand," *Vanity Fair*, May 2009 (online at http://www.vanityfair.com/politics/features/2009/05/iraqi-insurgents200905).

So if he didn't exist, the cliché is that we would have had to invent him. But the problem is we couldn't invent him. So it's not clear that the Awakening would have survived without his courage and his leadership. But there were a whole host of other factors. He was a necessary but not sufficient condition. We could not have succeeded without [Abu Musab al-] Zarqawi overreaching and ratcheting up the violence to medieval levels, which so alienated the other Sunni tribes. Generals [Raymond T.] Odierno and Petraeus revised the strategy, and the "surge" had a big impact. So there were a number of factors. Abdul Sattar was absolutely crucial, but he wasn't the only one.

In terms of the gentleman suggesting that we change our approach, I think the whole conceit of my writing the book was to try to get us to talk in a more adult and responsible fashion about having governments reach out to some of these nonstate actors. It is almost toxic in the United States, it is the third rail of politics to think that we are going to be talking to a whole bunch of people that really have done some pretty evil and despicable things. But the reality is that from time to time, it may make sense to do so. What the book aims to do is try to figure out when it is in our national interest, when it is not, be able to distinguish problems like we saw with Iran–Contra, but also try to identify opportunities in the future.[4]

The good news, I suppose, if you want to say a silver lining, is that there will be more opportunities for governments to make these decisions, to have these decision points in the future. Hopefully, they will be able to make them wisely.

Kilcullen: I agree very much with that. I would just add the comment that one of the big factors in 2007 was that we had finally sufficient troop density and sufficient people out on the ground to protect people that turned against al-Qaeda. Many people had tried to do that before and the consequences were fairly brutal. I think that was one of the major differences, as the ambassador pointed out.[5]

Question: Can you please shed some light on the difference between Taliban and

---

4 Mitchell B. Reiss, *Negotiating with Evil: When to Talk to Terrorists* (New York: Open Road Integrated Media, 2010 [e-book only]).

5 See David Kilcullen, "Reading Anbar," *American Interest*, September–October 2010, 94–98.

al-Qaeda? Didn't we support the Taliban while they were fighting the Soviet Union? Now they are fighting against us. This can happen in any other situation, a similar situation. Talking with them and supporting them can be taken as hypocrisy on our behalf.

Question: My question is about Hamas and current thinking that there was some opportunity at the time of the political process they engaged in, and the election that brought them to the Palestinian Legislative Council. Is there any kind of rethinking of that history and its aftermath, and thinking that maybe there was an opportunity to engage in a political way, given the process that has led to the election? And whether the demands of the Quartet[6] could have been brought to bear in a different way?

Question: With respect to Afghanistan, it doesn't seem like there's anybody that represents the entire insurgency. It's so fragmented. Would we be better off negotiating with insurgents at a local level? Is there something we can do to address individual, local community issues, and the grievances they have? Would that be a better strategy?

Hardy: Peter, for you experts and scholars, is it possible to disentangle the Taliban from al-Qaeda? Are they fish and fowl, or kindred spirits?

Peter R. Neumann: I think I'll leave that to David because he's the authority on this. But what I can say is that it seems very clear to me that there are three tests for whether there's a point in engaging with insurgents or terrorists or not.

The first test is, are they actually interested in engaging with us? Are they at a point in their military campaign where they believe they cannot win by military force alone, but at a point where they believe that engaging in compromise and engagement is actually more beneficial to them than to continue fighting? When we talk about engaging with terrorists, a lot of people who are enthusiastic about that always only ask, "Are we ready to engage?" But we also have to ask, "Are our opponents and adversaries ready to engage?"

---

6 The Quartet on the Middle East, often referred to simply as the Quartet, includes the United States, the United Nations, the European Union, and Russia.

The second test seems to be—and this draws on what David said about the Taliban—are the people that we are talking to actually capable of implementing any emerging peace agreement? That is incredibly difficult when you are dealing with a diffuse actor like the Taliban, which does not have clear command and control. The great thing about the IRA [Irish Republican Army] was that we knew that Gerry Adams and Martin McGuinness, over a period of time, would be able to bring their entire organization with them. That was the great advantage that we don't necessarily have with the Taliban or with al-Qaeda.

The third test is, are these groups geographically confined? The endgame in most of these engagement processes is to integrate them into some kind of political system. When you have a transnational actor like al-Qaeda, which is spread all over the world and based in no particular country, it is incredibly difficult to have an endgame that is based on integrating them in some kind of governance.

So I would always apply these three tests. Do they match yours, Mitch?

Reiss: Peter is absolutely right on this. The book goes on at some length to talk about these, using the case studies as evidence. But let's try to cycle back for a second about whether it makes sense to talk to the Taliban. From an American perspective right now, if you just take the four elements that I highlighted you need to have:

> • Are we defeating the Taliban on the battlefield or at least eroding their hope that they can be ultimately successful? I think David has already said that that probably isn't true.

> • Do we have sufficient intel assets to be able to peer into this group? Again, we have heard that they are not monolithic, they are splintered, [with] different leadership. Mullah [Mohammed] Omar is over the border [in Pakistan]; it's unclear how much he controls. Probably not the sort of intel assets we need in order to really prepare for negotiation.

• Do we have a partner for peace? Again, unclear whether we do or not.

• Do we have the patience to sustain the effort on the ground in order to deliver that hopelessness to them and also to sustain a diplomatic engagement that may last for many years? It's unclear whether the American people really have the stomach for that.

There are also other actors. We haven't monopolized the diplomatic process yet. Many governments are talking to the Taliban. It must be confusing for them. They are getting different messages all the time at different levels, from Afghanistan, from Pakistan, from us, from the Saudis, and from others.

Finally, you don't have to take my word for it; the head of the CIA [Leon E. Panetta] twice in the last week has been quoted as saying that he sees no evidence that the Taliban are really genuine about negotiating with us at this time.

Hardy: David, al-Qaeda was in Afghanistan in the 1990s. Are they in Afghanistan now?

Kilcullen: There is certainly some al-Qaeda presence in Afghanistan now, but it's very small numbers. We often hear a discussion about how we need to prevent al-Qaeda from moving back into Afghanistan if we were to leave. I think it's highly unlikely that they would abandon a very effective safe haven in Pakistan to go to Afghanistan. I think that's a little bit of a red herring.

I think where al-Qaeda comes into the issue in Afghanistan is that we care about the Taliban because they make Afghanistan unstable. We care about Afghanistan being unstable because it's part of a broader regional pattern of instability that includes Pakistan, and in Pakistan we have over a hundred nuclear weapons, a fragile state, and al-Qaeda headquarters. So that's where it comes in. It's a sort of second- or third-order effect of failure in Afghanistan, that we would see a potential state collapse and access to nuclear weapons on the part of al-Qaeda. But I think in terms of day by day, it's not such a critical issue on the ground in Afghanistan.

I would just offer a comment also on Mitchell's point. One of the things that can happen—and it happened to us in Iraq, but I would argue it happened to us by accident—is you can get into a situation where you've got a virtuous circle, where the better you target and kill the irreconcilable minority, the more willing everybody else is to reconcile with you. And the better the deal you offer to everybody else, the more isolated the last few irreconcilables become, so you can actually accelerate a process of movement toward peace by the way you both negotiate and target at the same time. That is certainly what happened in 2007–8 in Iraq, and it is certainly being talked about as something that we might try to do in Afghanistan right now. My only concern would be, I was there, I was part of the planning process in Iraq, [and] I'm not quite sure we know how we did it in Iraq. So I'm not sure we can pull it off again.

Malley: I think there were two moments, when it comes to Hamas, that were moments where we could have gone in a different direction. One was elections in 2006, which were immediately followed by the Quartet conditions, and the other was the sort of Mecca agreement made in 2007, which was accompanied by a decision by many—including by many Palestinians—that the best thing to do was to thwart it and to ensure that it wouldn't last long. There is a lot of debate about it in Europe. I know many European officials who now question the choices they made back then. I don't know that there's that much here, but I think certainly in Europe and in the United Nations and elsewhere, people are wondering whether it was the right approach. I want to suggest a few quick things about it.

I think it was costly after 2006 in terms of the message of support for democracy, and I think it was costly in terms of our being able to influence Hamas, which was, divided may be too strong a word, but there was a trend that was more interested in politics, and one that had opposed participation in elections for a long time and then finally acquiesced or lost that debate. I think that because of the choices that were made after 2006 and 2007, it has hardened a certain view within Hamas, and of course it has given democracy a bad name in quite a few places around the region.

I don't want to sound naïve. I don't know whether if one were to change policy toward Hamas—and again, it doesn't necessarily mean talking to them, though it could—I'm not sure Hamas could change in a way that people would like them to change. What I do know is that what has been done so far has not put them to the test. The Quartet conditions are conditions that no official in Hamas could even come close to thinking of accepting because they go to the core of the ideology rather than to the more nuanced area of practice. I always thought that is what we should have done. The conditions we should have put is a real cease-fire in the West Bank and Gaza and acceptance of a process or endorsing President [Mahmoud] Abbas's ability to negotiate on behalf of all Palestinians, and then to put an agreement to referendum, and to acquiesce in the outcome of that referendum. That seemed to me to be more logical; both more meaningful in some ways, and a harder test for Hamas to turn down. It would have created tensions within the movement. By putting the three conditions that the Quartet put, which may make sense theoretically, we spared them the need to come to terms with their own views.

Question: David Kilcullen, I totally agreed with your presentation. I thought it excellently set out the need for a carefully targeted military posture that would encourage bottom-up peace. I'd like to invite you to say a bit about the economic posture that needs to be adopted as well. I'm thinking mainly of Afghanistan, but I think it's widely applicable. Foreign aid can enormously reduce the incentives for peace, both because it artificially promotes some communities at the expense of others, and because it actually can be seen as, in a strange way, a reward for continued conflict, for as long as it's seen as tied to a crisis which when it ends, so does the foreign aid. I'd like to invite you to add a little point on that.

Question: Mr. Kilcullen, in an ideal scenario where we start to engage from the bottom up or community-based level, what would be the role of the military, and how would they support this type of engagement?

Hardy: You don't all have to make final remarks, but it's your chance to make them. Peter, do you want to add anything?

Neumann: I'm fine.

Hardy: Rob?

Malley: Just one thing, on a very interesting intervention I heard today from the other panelists. I think the message I get is what Mitchell Reiss said earlier. I think we need to demystify this question. There may be cases where different approaches are necessary, but to demystify it, turn it less into the toxic issue it has become, particularly in the cases that I have worked on, but I'm sure it's true in others as well. Any shift in our current policy—which I believe is failing, at least in the two instances I work on most— any shift is a betrayal of our principles, any shift is a betrayal of our allies. I think there are many different ways we could go about it which would be better for us and better for them.

Kilcullen: I don't have any follow-up remarks, but I might just answer those two questions. In terms of economic posture, there is a lot of research out there, ranging from Dambisa Moyo, a Kenyan World Bank economist, through Bill Easterley, Paul Collier, various other people, suggesting that aid often does have a destabilizing effect.[7] In fact, any influx of cash into an underdeveloped economy is likely to have a destabilizing effect, regardless of the origin. I think what we found in places like Afghanistan and Iraq is that community-based investments, such as, for example, the World Bank's National Solidarity Program in Afghanistan, have done a lot better than large-scale international donor programs.

But I would even tend to suggest that we move out of the concept of aid to a broader

---

7 Dambisa Moyo, *Dead Aid: Why Aid is Not Working and How There is Another Way for Africa* (New York: Farrar, Straus and Giroux, 2009); William Easterly, *The White Man's Burden: Why the West's Efforts to Aid the Rest Have Done So Much Ill and So Little Good* (New York: Penguin Press, 2006); Paul Collier, *The Bottom Billion: Why the Poorest Countries are Failing and What Can Be Done About It* (New York: Oxford University Press, 2007).

concept of aid, trade, and investment, where investing in private-sector new company formation at the local level seems to be much more effective in generating ownership with communities. There are a lot of examples where we give people a power plant and the Taliban come along and blow it up because it's a symbol of the government. If you sell it to them, the Taliban aren't going to blow it up, and if they try, the locals are going to fight them. It is a completely different model. But you have to do that in a fair trade way which works with communities on a good basis.

In fact, one of the most important roles of the international assistance programs is to provide economic support to allow Western businesses to do deals in these areas with some guarantee of some kind of return, and in a way that isn't punitive toward the interests of local peoples. So it is sort of upstream pricing support and regulatory support that we can provide. Lots of other things to say about that; it's a whole other topic.

In terms of military posture, I think the most important thing the military can do to enable this kind of thing is to stay the hell out of these situations. If you do go in, then I think you need to think about yourself in terms of dealing with instability rather than dealing with enemies. You need to approach the problem of instability as the problem rather than try to identify individual actors and kill them, and sort of assume if I just kill this guy, the problem of instability is going to go away. It doesn't really work like that.

You need to take a posture where you say, all right, there are 300 problems in this district. It's Afghanistan or Iraq, so probably 90 percent of them can't be fixed, and they certainly can't be fixed by some dude who doesn't even come from here, so let's triage down to problems that are actually creating instability, that are actually being exploited by violent actors, that we can do something about in a meaningful time frame with the resources we have available. You usually find one or two carefully focused, limited interventions that have a much better result. I mean, if you went into Kentucky and tried to disarm the population, you'd probably have some significant problems. You go into Anbar and try to do that, the result is history.

Reiss: I think it's very important for policy makers to have some humility. I was down at CENTCOM[8] doing some research, talking to a very senior official there who was speaking glowingly of all the progress that was taking place in Afghanistan. After about 15 or 20 minutes of this, he stopped and wanted my reaction. I said, "I certainly hope you're right, but you've got to remember, we've been working on the D.C. school system for 30 years." We just have to be a little bit more modest in terms of what we think we can accomplish, especially in foreign cultures, foreign societies, people whose languages we don't speak and whose ways we don't understand.

---

8 U.S. Central Command, the joint command that oversees U.S. military interests in the Middle East and Central Asia, is based at MacDill Air Force Base in Tampa, Florida.

Lebanese Armenians rip down a billboard of Turkish Prime Minister Recep Tayyip Erdoğan in Martyr's Square in Beirut during Erdoğan's visit to Lebanon, November 25, 2010. Turkey is seeking a broader role in the Middle East but has a long history to overcome in some areas. (Corbis/EPA/Wael Hamzeh)

Part Three

Shifting Regional Dynamics:
Turkey, Israel, Iran, and the
Arab States

CHAPTER ELEVEN

TURKEY'S MIDDLE EAST POLICY

ÖMER TAŞPINAR

What I will try to do is give an overview of Turkey's Middle East policy and in what ways we should try to analyze this shifting dynamic in the region. Let me start with the domestic dynamics in Turkey and try to talk about some of the drivers of Turkey's new activist, engagement-oriented foreign policy.

The big question in Washington and Western capitals is whether this is an Islamization of Turkey. There is a certain preconceived notion of Turkey as a staunch ally of the United States, a country that had during the Cold War an almost exclusively pro-Western attitude which did not really look to the Middle East as an area where Turkish leverage or power, or Turkish economic relations, really mattered.

I think in many ways, instead of seeing this through the lens of Islamization, I would submit to you that this is rather a normalization of Turkish identity, Turkish state-society relations, and in many ways also a certain level of democratization. Public opinion began to matter more in the last 10 years in Turkey. I think that is a product of democratization. Turkey overall, despite the fact that it is not really a liberal democracy yet by the European standard, is becoming a more democratic country where public opinion really matters. That means that overall, the elite-oriented structure of Turkish foreign policy, and the military-oriented structure of Turkish foreign policy, is changing. Public opinion and a new elite, a different kind of elite—not the Kemalist elite, but a more conservative elite, the rise of an Anatolian elite—is also a major driver of this change in Turkey.

105

Is it Islamization? In many ways, it is more of a conservative Turkey that is emerging, a more nationalist Turkey, I would say a more independent actor. I would underline this concept of independence. I think both the Turkish military and the current government in Turkey, the AKP,[1] agree that Turkey should be more of an independent actor, that it should not really pursue a foreign policy that is exclusively pro-West, oriented toward the transatlantic dynamics, or toward the East. It should basically pursue its own national and economic interests.

That brings me to the second driver of Turkish foreign policy toward the Middle East: the economy. When you look at the trade figures, Turkey's commerce and trade with the Middle East has quadrupled in the last 10 years. You have more and more Turkish businessmen, more and more Turkish private-sector companies—construction companies—active in the Arab world and the Middle East. This is also something very different in the post-Cold War dynamic. During the Cold War, the Middle East was not really open to Turkish markets, and Turkish businessmen really did not look at the Middle East as a market. But this is increasingly changing, and there is a diversification of Turkey's export markets. Russia, Central Asia, and the Middle East are part of these shifting dynamics of Turkish export orientation. Although Europe is still the main market, there is more and more trade with the Middle East. I think this is a driver, a kind of mercantilistic driver if you will, of Turkey's approach to the Middle East.

There is also the fact that Turkey is coming to terms with its Muslim identity. The government in power comes from an Islamic pedigree. Some people argue that it is still a pro-Islamic government, and in many ways, there is a sense of solidarity with the Middle East, there is a sense of solidarity with the Arab world. It is not really a vision that is present in the Kemalist circles, which tend to look at the Arab world as an area which is backward and does not really matter for Turkey's strategic interests. To the contrary, I think the current government and its grand vision—especially the one of Foreign

---

1 Adalet ve Kalkınma Partisi (AKP), which translates as the Justice and Development Party.

Minister Ahmet Davutoglu—believes that during the Cold War, Turkey's obsession with Westernization and belonging to Western clubs came at the expense of Turkey's Muslim identity, Turkey's strategic depth potentially with the Middle East and Central Asia, with Africa. So you have a more 360-degree foreign policy emerging in Turkey.

Those are some of the positive drivers. Starting with the end of the Cold War, the Kurdish problem was a more negative driver of Turkish foreign policy in the Middle East. If you focus on the 1990s and look at the way Turkish foreign policy toward the Middle East was shaped, it was almost exclusively focused on the Kurdish question. This is at the heart of why Turkey in fact decided not to support the U.S. invasion of Iraq, because the Turkish security establishment, the Turkish political establishment, and definitely Turkish parliamentarians had a simple question to ask for American policy makers: what is your vision of Iraq once Saddam [Hussein] is gone? And especially, what is your vision of northern Iraq—the Kurds—once Saddam is gone? Once they realized that the answer was not clear—that there was a vague answer along the lines of Iraq will become democratic, and there will be power-sharing mechanisms, and people will find a way—the Turkish emphasis on the status quo and stability in Iraq kicked in. There emerged a major debate about whether the Kurds would achieve independence in a post-Saddam Iraq. So the Kurdish question dominated a great part of the 1990s and the early part of the 21st century's first decade. From 2003 to 2006, Turkey's approach to the Kurdish question was exclusively security-oriented.

What happened in the last four or five years is that Turkey decided to change its policy toward the Kurdish question. That also helped change Turkey's image in the Arab world. I think in the Arab world there were a number of preconceived notions of Turkey. First, that Turkey would never say no to the United States, that it was basically a lackey of the United States, and whatever the United States would ask, Turkey would do. The fact that Turkey voted against the invasion of Iraq, and against the participation of Turkish troops, and to allow U.S. troops to pass through Turkey was a big surprise, not only in the Arab world, but also in the West. But in a way it conflicted with this image of a pro-U.S. Turkey that would always be pliant to U.S. demands.

Then the image of Turkey as the anti-Kurdish country, Turkey as the country that would always suppress the Kurds, began to change in the last four or five years. How? With basically this approach to the domestic dimension, and the foreign policy dimension, of the Kurdish question. Turkey simply decided, in the last four years I believe, that it would be better to co-opt northern Iraqi Kurds rather than confront them, to in a way play big brother to them, to tell them that they can coexist with Turkey as long as they don't provide safe havens for the PKK, the Kurdish rebel organization.[2] In that sense, a new modus vivendi, a new partnership emerged between Irbil and Ankara. Turkey began engaging not only former rivals like Syria, but also northern Iraq, on the question of the Kurds. That brought a new soft-power dimension to Turkey's perception in the Middle East, which was usually more along the lines of hard power and Turkish military and repressive attitudes toward the Kurds.

So that also is an important factor, the possibility for Turkey to transcend the Kurdish problem, to find ways to deal with the cultural and political dimension of the problem at home with democratization, and the ability to deal with the foreign policy dimension of this with northern Iraq by engaging northern Iraq instead of confronting it, by accepting that there is a Kurdish federation. Coming to terms with the Kurdish reality also is an important shifting dynamic in Turkey's approach to the Middle East.

I'd like to also look at the way that Turks look at Iran. This is obviously the most important issue as far as recent news is concerned, and the debate in Washington is concerned. Let's not forget that Turkey is a Sunni country. Turkey has a perception of this "rise of the Shi'ite" and is also showing a sense of solidarity to a certain degree with the Sunni Arab world in terms of sharing concerns about the rise of a "Shi'ite crescent," as

---

2 Partiya Karkerên Kurdistan (PKK), the Kurdistan Workers' Party.

it came to be called. In that sense, this may contradict with Turkey's perception in Washington that it is a country that always defends Iran and refuses to partner with the United States in terms of applying sanctions to Iran.

I think deep down, there is a big debate within the Turkish government about Iran. There are those who argue that Turkey should engage in a containment strategy against Iran and try to basically de-link Syria from Iran. That is almost official policy. The attempt to basically split Syria from Iran is part of this Turkish vision of trying to contain Iran. Turkey also does not want Iraq to be under the domination of Iran. This is why Turkey has been very supportive of Iraqiya and [Ayad] Allawi. Ankara is not very happy with the way things are going in Iraq, with [Nouri al-] Maliki emerging as a force that would continue, to a certain degree, Iran's influence over Iraq. So you can see areas like Syria and Iraq where Turkey is concerned about Iranian influence.

Turkey is also concerned about Iran monopolizing Hamas and Hezbollah. This is why you have seen leaders like [Hamas leader] Khaled Meshaal visit Ankara, where Turkey clearly wanted to give a message to Khaled Meshaal that there are other ways to look at the region, that Hamas should not put all its foreign policy vision into the Syrian or, more importantly, Iranian basket but should look at Turkey and how Turkey can also help in terms of changing Hamas's vision. I think the messages given to Hamas were essentially messages that wanted to tame or moderate Hamas's ideology, Hamas's stance toward Israel. So we can also put Turkey's policy in Lebanon and with the Palestinians and Hamas as attempts to contain Iranian influence.

On the other hand, Turkey is very concerned about Israel and the United States using coercive diplomacy, or down the line resorting to military action against Iran. Turkey, if there is one lesson we should keep in mind, is a status-quo power. Turkey does not want destabilization in the Middle East. The way Turks look at Iran at this point is through a lens of what happened in Iraq. Another war in the region, one that would target Iran, even if it is just surgical strikes to nuclear sites, would in the eyes of Turkey totally destabilize the region. This is why Turkey is not willing to go down the road of coercive diplomacy with Iran. This is why I think Turkey does not want to support diplomatic coercion and economic sanctions. Turkey wants exclusively an engagement policy with Iran. It does not believe in the effectiveness of sanctions, it does not believe in the effectiveness of coercive diplomacy. More importantly, I think Ankara believes that there is this almost domino effect, that once you start on the road of coercive diplomacy, unavoidably, this may lead to the next step of taking military action. That was the lesson of Iraq, and I think there is a lot to be learned from the way that Turks look at the 1990s and Iraq for how they look at Iran today, and how similar dynamics of coercive diplomacy and sanctions may lead down the road to military action against a regime.

This is why I think Turkey is torn between containing Iran—the urge to contain Iran, the urge to show its Sunni credentials to its Arab partners—and the need to also engage Iran, to avoid playing to what Turkey sees as the American camp or the transatlantic camp of coercive diplomacy.

Finally, with Israel, I think it is important to emphasize that public opinion really matters in Turkey. The golden age of Turkey–Israel relations was at a time when the military was much more active in Turkey and public opinion did not matter that much. Now that we have a different government in Turkey, one that has populist instincts, one that really looks at opinion polls in Turkey, the absence of a Middle East peace process is a major problem for Ankara.

The golden years of Turkish–Israeli partnership were in 1996–97, when the military partnership treaty was signed. But even then, public opinion had a hard time to digest this. It was essentially military-to-military relations, or elite-to-elite relations, that was the driver of relations with Israel. The minute Turkey and the Turkish public opinion realized there is no peace process, the minute Turkish public opinion realized that there is a more hawkish Israeli government, things started to change in the calculation of Turkey.

Nevertheless, just two years ago, Turkey was trying hard to provide some bridge between Syria and Israel, for instance. Despite this image of Turkey now as this very anti-Israel country, let's not forget that as late as 2008, Shimon Peres was addressing the Turkish parliament and Turkey was trying very hard to mediate between Syria and Israel. This is also part of Turkey's new engagement policy, trying to revitalize the peace process so that you can sell the partnership with Israel to your public opinion. If there are Israeli jets bombing Lebanon or Gaza, it is very hard for a Turkish prime minister who really cares about public opinion, who has populist rather than Islamist (I believe) instincts, to defend the partnership. On top of this, after what happened with the *Mavi Marmara* incident, I think it will be very hard to return to any kind of golden era. Normalization would be a major achievement within itself.

This is why I think it is crucial for Turkey to see that there is a Middle East peace process. Otherwise, the same jets that were bombing Hamas and Lebanon, I don't think they will once again be able to train in Turkey with the Turkish military. This would be something too hard to swallow for Turkish domestic public opinion.

I will conclude with this: public opinion really matters. What we see in Turkey, rather than Islamization, in my opinion, is a more independent foreign policy, a more nationalist foreign policy, a foreign policy that does not want to put all its eggs into the Western basket. It is a more diversified foreign policy, and it is also a foreign policy that is mercantilistic, that emphasizes the new markets and new trade relations.

Turkey sees a power vacuum in the Middle East. Egypt is no longer able to provide the leadership role, and Turkey has become, with its soft power and self-confidence and its booming economy, a country that can provide some leadership in the region. It is up to Washington, in my opinion, to realize whether this new Turkish soft power in the region can be leveraged according to U.S. national interests. The choice for American policy makers is whether they should confront Turkey—punish Turkey for some of its policies vis-à-vis Iran and Israel—or try to engage, leverage, and co-opt Turkey. I would conclude that this is a very difficult choice.

CHAPTER TWELVE

THE RISING IRAN?

ALEX VATANKA

I am going to focus on Iran. I hope you don't mind, on this day of the 31st anniversary of the hostage situation in Tehran, I'm going to stay away from U.S.–Iran relations. I am instead going to look at Iran's regional affairs.

When I saw the title of the panel here, "Shifting Regional Dynamics," I said to myself, everybody knows what sorts of shifts have taken place in the Middle East in recent years. What can I bring to the table in 15 minutes that might be worth something? Frankly, right away, the issue that came to mind was to highlight the debate inside Iran about the country's regional policies, its successes and failures. So that is what I'm going to try to do, to talk about that debate. It might surprise you, the extent of that debate inside Iran about where the country is going in terms of its regional policy. It might come as a surprise to those of you who look at Iran as a dictatorship or semi-dictatorship.

But before I get to that, let me say a few words about what I heard again and again yesterday—and I think to some extent it is true—this notion of the "rising" Iran. I don't think anyone would dispute the fact that Iran's regional power has increased substantially over the last 10 years, particularly following the downfall of the regime of Saddam Hussein. There is no doubt about it. But I think we have to be careful and qualify. It is easy for us to make the assumption that here is Iran, unstoppable, on the march across different arenas in the Middle East, and there is nothing that can be done about it.

If you look at those arenas in the Middle East where Iran is strongest—for instance, in Iraq or Lebanon, or among Palestinians for that matter—it seems to me that Iran has the kind of leverage that it has because of something that it didn't do. In the case of Iraq, it was direct U.S. action that resulted in Iran having the kind of clout that it has today. In the case of Iranian influence with Hamas in Gaza or Hezbollah in Lebanon, it is as a result of what we heard again and again yesterday from the distinguished visitors from the Middle East: the lack of progress in the Arab–Israeli peace talks. And Ömer [Taşpınar] just mentioned this in relation to Turkey, that the Turks are now trying to fill the vacuum, when there is a vacuum. Ömer specifically mentioned Egypt. But it seems to me that Iran has been playing the same role, filling vacuums in the case of Lebanese Shi'a and some of the rejectionist Sunni elements in the Palestinian territories.

That is a reality of geopolitics in the Middle East, Iran playing that sort of role, going in and helping entities that are looking for sponsors. That is not to say that Iran has many options in terms of going around and spreading its patronage. I don't really see a lot of takers out there, and I think that is what has to get us to think about that, qualifying the notion. When we say "Iran on the rise," are we talking about Iran on the rise across the board? Or are we talking specific places where there are people who are desperate for sponsorship and Iran has been able to play that role?

I'll put it to you another way. The attractiveness of the Islamic Republic as a model, again, when I look at the debate in Iraq today, some six years after the downfall of the Ba'athist regime, I don't see a lot of loud voices in that country arguing for the concept of the *velayat-e faqih*, the supreme jurisprudent. I don't see that model being advocated that strongly in places like Lebanon, either. What I see is those takers, those entities in the Middle East that are in need of sponsorship, looking to Iran for financial and other tangible support. That by far outweighs the sort of attractiveness of the Iranian ideology, if there is one.

114

From my point of view, it is premature to say [President Mahmoud] Ahmedinejad and [Supreme Leader Ali] Khamenei—and we've seen some headlines to that regard in recent years—that they have won the future of the Middle East, that the future of the Middle East will look as it does in Iran today. I think that is premature and we need to qualify that.

With that said, let me switch over to the internal debate in Iran about the country's regional policy. Before I say anything on this, let me just point out that, again, there is a very lively debate in Iran about all things related to the policy-making process, including foreign and regional policies. There are taboos or semi-taboos. The two that come to mind are U.S.–Iran relations, which is really a red line, and so is the nuclear program. Those two issues are kind of taboo; you don't touch them because the supreme leader's office and his people are the ones who are in charge. Any kind of debate is seen to be undermining the official position, hence you don't have that kind of debate.

When it comes to the regional policy of Iran, you have a very lively debate. I just reminded myself when I was going through the literature preparing for today about the sort of common consensus that seems to be there. Again, it might surprise you, but overall, when you look at the literature that exists, and look away from regime apologists who will defend anything the authorities in Tehran do, the consensus is that Iran's standing in the region is weak. They say this publicly, and you can go to various sources that debate and research these issues, and that seems to be the consensus.

Let me tell you why they keep saying it's weak. There are two things that come up all the time when they talk about Iran's weakness on regional policy. One is that its basic assessment of regional dynamics is wrong. The other thing is that Iran's policy performance is contradictory.

What do I mean by that? The primary issue that seems to come up is that the Iranian authorities continue—and this is a regime that has been in place for 31 years now—continue to have this hope, although they don't publicly state it, but this is something that most people agree seems to be the hope in the top echelons in power in Iran: that the regimes around them in the Arab world will fall apart—that the House of Saud will fall apart tomorrow, that the small GCC [Gulf Cooperation Council] states will sort of disappear, and new entities will emerge. This seems to be the wrong assessment that critics of the regime keep referring to.

The other one is this notion of pursuing a contradictory policy. To give you the big picture, on the one hand you have slogans that we hear on a daily basis coming out from various agencies in Iran, talking about a Middle East without extraterritorial powers being involved. That is a clear reference to the United States and the West in general. So they want—and they are open about it—they want the United States to pull out. They want the U.S. Navy's Fifth Fleet to pull out, and they want to be able to go ahead and rearrange the security framework of that region. It is contradictory because they clearly are misunderstanding the point or trying to ignore the reality that most of those Arab states to the south of the Persian Gulf look at their security totally tied to the presence of the United States. This is what Iranian critics keep highlighting. It cannot be done that way, you cannot tell the states on the other side of the Gulf or in Egypt and so forth that you are looking for partnership with them while you at the same time undermine them by asking them to disassociate themselves with something—a U.S. presence—that in their view guarantees their security.

In other words, what I think the critics of the regime in Iran are saying is that Iran needs to start thinking about reducing this confidence deficit. It is doing a very poor job trying to deliver on this front.

Since we talked about Turkey, let me also make a quick comparison here between Iranian foreign policy in action under the ruling elite headed by President Ahmadinejad and show you where Iran, even with these contradictions that I just outlined, still has been able to perform slightly better in recent years, significantly better when it comes to its relations with Turkey, at least when you compare it to its relations with the Arab states.

We heard from Ömer that relations for the Turks with the Middle East have improved significantly. For Iran, it has been an amazing improvement. If you look back from 2000 to today, you see a major transformation in Iran's behavior toward Turkey and in terms of its interactions with Turkey. Some people would say that is down to AKP[1] coming to power in 2002; that there is some sort of pan-Islamist agenda going on, that the Islamist-leaning AKP and the ruling elite in Iran have some sort of ideological platform they share. Actually, I think that's just a headline, and if you look at the realities of what is bringing these two neighboring states together, it is the tangible benefits they have been able to achieve as a result of their cooperation, namely the fight against Kurdish militants and energy and economic cooperation. Iran's trade with Turkey has gone from about $1 billion to over $10 billion in 10 years. When you look at the dialogue between Iran and Turkey, the role of Islam—Sunni or Shi'a—does not really come into the picture. You might have Ahmadinejad show up in a mosque in Istanbul, but that is not really what brings these two countries together.

These tangible benefits are, arguably, cementing relations between Iran and Turkey. If you compare that to Iran's relations with the Arab states, particularly the ones in the pro–U.S. column, you see Iran taking baby steps toward reaching out. For instance, you have energy and trade discussions in place at all times. But nothing substantive has come out of it as a result of years of negotiations.

To my mind, the reason for that is very simple, and I want to go back to the point I made earlier. The Iranians are trying to get to these Arab states selling themselves as partners while at the same time saying they want to rearrange the security framework in the region. It just doesn't seem to be able to work for them, and to my mind, that is not a surprise at all.

---

1 Adalet ve Kalkınma Partisi (AKP), which translates as the Justice and Development Party.

Let me start rounding up and say something about Iran as a nation-state. When we talk about Iran on the rise, I think it is very legitimate when you look at it from an Iranian perspective to say if the West in general wants Iran to be weak and not be involved in any arena in the Middle East, that is not going to happen. That's not going to happen for Ahmadinejad, that's not going to happen for Mir Hussein Mousavi and the Green opposition movement. You could have a secular nationalist regime in Tehran; some of their desires for being able to project power will not change. The same as we witnessed over the last 40 years, the transformation from Iran under the Shah to the Islamic Republic—some of the basic interests remain the same. I think that will continue to be the case.

But what I think is very interesting, and perhaps the West can help this debate inside Iran through its action, is there is this divide inside Iran. Right now it is between the opposition and the hard-line ruling elite about what is the best way of promoting Iran's regional interests. It is so obvious when you compare the performance from 1997 to 2005 of President Mohammad Khatami, who made such great headway in terms of building confidence across the board, particularly with the Arab states (and by the way, the golden period in relations with Turkey started on his watch, five years before Ahmadinejad came to power). If you compare what Khatami was able to do, compare that to what Ahmadinejad has done since 2005—since he came to power, we have heard a lot of revolutionary talk coming from the presidential palace in Tehran—but when you look at tangible achievements on a regional level, we have seen very little (in my humble argument) except the strategic outposts in places like Lebanon or with Hamas in Gaza and so forth. On top of that, you have what they are selling to us—those who are observing Iran's performance—these relations with countries as far away as Venezuela, Bolivia, and Mozambique.

My point is we had in Khatami someone who was looking at the national interests of Iran and was working (from my perspective) rationally, trying to achieve certain tangible benefits for Iran. In the case of Ahmadinejad, we see revolutionary talk, we see abstract notions about Iran becoming a global power, and so forth. The debate in Iran is while Mr. Hugo Chávez [of Venezuela] has visited Tehran eight times over the last few years, not a single Arab leader from any of the large Arab states, with the exception of [Syrian President] Bashar al-Assad, has actually been to Tehran. So if anything, we have seen a return back to the bad old days in Iranian–Arab relations.

And financial loss—when you hear about Iran building up factories in Venezuela or investing in various things, reconstruction in Lebanon, there is a debate in Iran about where the country's national resources are going. That is a very interesting debate when you bear in mind that the country is under sanctions right now, and the sanctions are starting to have an impact. I wonder if those realities will perhaps make Iran less adventurous.

Finally, let me say this. I've talked about the debate, that was the core of the talk. But as you all know, those people who are arguing against the government on these issues are having a very tough time right now politically in Iran. They are under pressure. They are not part of the bloc that shapes policy. But that doesn't mean the U.S. and her allies in the region should ignore these deep-seated Iranian desires that I think are very prevalent across the political spectrum except, as I said, the Ahmadinejad–Khamenei bloc that controls the levers of power today. Right now, popular Iranian nationalism is working against Ahmadinejad and Khamenei. At least that is my view; it is definitely working against the regime. Whatever the U.S. does—and that is also true for pro-U.S. Arab allies—it has to bear in mind that policies that go against what are inherently genuine national interests of Iran, if they are done in that manner, then you will push that force of nationalism into the hands of the Ahmadinejads of this world. That is something, from a Western and U.S. point of view, that should be avoided.

CHAPTER THIRTEEN

ISRAEL'S PERSPECTIVE ON THE BROADER MIDDLE EAST

ITAMAR RABINOVICH

I will try to share with you the perspective from Jerusalem, or in my case from Tel Aviv, on the Middle East chessboard, or regional system. I'd like to preface it with three observations.

One, the 20th century was an exceptional century for the Middle East in the sense that the two successor states to the imperial powers that had dominated the region in earlier centuries, Turkey and Iran, were very much outside the mainstream of the politics of the region. Turkey was looking westward, to Europe mostly, and Iran was preoccupied with the Soviet threat, with regional issues, and on the whole did not play a major role in the politics of the Middle East. That began to change with the Iranian revolution of 1979 and has changed in recent years as the direction of Turkish policy has changed. We now have these two major states very much, not just in the politics of the Middle East, but trying to shape and to some extent dominate the politics of the Middle East. That has made a very significant change in the regional setting of the Middle East.

Second, from an Israeli point of view, in the late 1950s we ran regional policy under the heading of "the orientation toward the periphery." This was Israel in the Middle East of the 1950s, the height of the Arab–Israeli conflict, no prospect of an Arab–Israeli settlement, the sense of ongoing Arab hostility. Israel under [Prime Minister] David Ben-Gurion at that time was looking for allies and props for conducting foreign policy. It looked beyond the immediate circle around Israel, and it saw other pro-Western, anti-communist countries feeling threatened by the wave of revolutionary pan–Arab nationalism, led by [Egyptian President] Gamal Abdel Nasser. They looked to Turkey, they looked at Iran, they looked at Ethiopia. With the blessing of the [Dwight D.] Eisenhower administration, they constructed a tacit alliance. That was a very close alliance at the time. (Turkey and Iran of course are not peripheral countries, but if you think that the core area of the Middle East is the Arab–Israeli part of the Middle East, then Turkey and Iran seem to be on the periphery of the region, hence the nickname.)

In a way, this has been reversed. In the peace processes of the 1970s and 1990s, Israel made peace with Egypt and Jordan, went to mutual recognition with Palestinian nationalism, and went quite a way toward at least sketching what the Israeli–Syrian peace would look like. It was coming to terms with its immediate environment. What we have seen in the last two decades is that the former allies, Iran and Turkey, are drifting away, in the case of Iran, to open, virulent hostility; and in the case of Turkey, to a somewhat more ambivalent but certainly not friendly orientation. Not that we have fully come to terms with the immediate circle around us, but we definitely have lost the ability to interact with the external circle.

The third observation: 20 or 30 years ago, when one thought about the Middle East, one thought primarily about the Arab world. They were never identical terms, but to a great extent, they were coterminous or overlapping terms. Clearly, this is not the case now, with the entry of two major Muslim but not Arab states, Iran and Turkey, each of them with more than 70 million people, large economies, very sophisticated elites, and large military powers. The balance of power in the region has shifted. You have three powerful non–Arab actors, not at peace with one another, but still non–Arab actors—Turkey, Iran, Israel. So it is a much more complex Middle Eastern arena than used to be the case.

Let me look at how Israelis analyze and understand what we have just heard from two speakers: the changes in Turkish policy, and the Iranian policy.

The Iranian challenge is clear. From a very close alliance with the Iran of the Shah, we moved to a very hostile attitude by the revolutionary regime. I would say if Israel arranges by priority its list of threats, the threat from Iran is number one. Not necessarily or not just in the nuclear sense; I think Iran wants the role of hegemonic power, it wants to be a regional hegemon. It began with a genuine effort that every major revolution has tried in the past—the French, the Russians, later the Iranians—to export the revolution, mostly to countries with large Shi'a communities. Later on, as the original revolutionary impulse died, we are now dealing with a regime trying to establish regional hegemony, and not without successes. Lebanon is pretty much, through Hezbollah, under the boot; significant bases in the Mediterranean, both in Lebanon and in Gaza; the relationship with Hamas. Syria used to be an ally and partner, and I would say it changed under [Syrian President] Bashar al-Assad from a relationship of equals to more of a patron-client relationship between Iran and Syria. Of course we need to look closely at what happens in Iraq after the American withdrawal, and what level of influence Iran will have over the Iraqi regime as it emerges out of the American occupation. That is definitely a challenge.

I would look at the nuclear issue in this context more in the sense of a nuclear umbrella. I was trying to think of what the current Iranian regime would do in the region when it has a nuclear umbrella. Countries that have a nuclear umbrella are not attacked. Had Saddam Hussein waited a few more years in 1990, Kuwait would still be occupied Iraqi territory because he would have had nuclear weapons. So as I see it, in the context of this panel, the quest for nuclear power is the quest for a nuclear umbrella that would further beef up the Iranian quest for hegemony.

On Turkey, I have a slightly different take than Mr. [Ömer] Taşpınar, in the following way. I think that people sometimes call it neo–Ottomanism. There is a sense that since being rebuffed by Europe, Turkey wants to build a position in its region. Not being really part of Europe sends you somewhat to the Caucasus, to Central Asia, but also to the very promising lands of the Middle East. The current Turkish regime sees a potential for building assets and influence. Public opinion is a factor, but the government in many cases has galvanized public opinion. It has not necessarily always been on the receiving end of public opinion, as we have seen that it also galvanizes public opinion.

Let me also mention an interesting document that I don't think has been officially published but is in the works—the "red book," the annual report prepared by the Turkish national security council. The national security council now represents a different composition than it had in earlier days when it was dominated by the military. Israel is not mentioned as an enemy in that book, but it is mentioned several times, which has not been the case in the past. Iran is not mentioned as a national security threat. Clearly, there is a major shift in the way Turkey sees and acts in the region.

Iran has managed to build a coalition—call it the camp of resistance—composed of itself, Syria, Hamas, and Hezbollah. It is anti–American, anti–Israeli, anti-peace process as we know it. Turkey has not joined that coalition, but certainly some of its activities reinforce that coalition and reinforce the direction in which it is trying to take the region.

If you look at it from the Israeli perspective, they are not good developments, not encouraging developments. What do you do about that? Number one is the peace process. Moving on in the peace process, completing the negotiations with the Palestinians and moving in parallel or subsequently to a renewed negotiation with Syria, is something that many Israelis, myself included, believe in. It is good for Israel, for Israel's own good reasons. It is also helpful and essential for dealing with this new regional equation, because if Iran leads the camp of resistance contrary to the peace process, you want to help the camp that is supportive of the peace process—Egypt, Saudi Arabia, other conservative or moderate Arab states, and the Palestinian Authority (as distinct from Hamas). If there is no peace process, this camp—which is not very powerful anyway—suffers. If there is a peace process and they have something to show for it, something to rally around, it is easier for them to cooperate, if not openly, at least tacitly, with Israel and certainly with the United States. So moving on in the peace process is one element.

Second, Turkey can have a role in the peace process. It was mentioned that in 2008–9, Turkey mediated between Israel and Syria. That may not have been the most successful part of the long Israeli–Syrian peace process, but Turkey enjoyed that role.

At the end of the day, this negotiation needs to be managed by the United States, mostly for one reason: Syria is not interested in peace with Israel itself, it is interested in peace with Washington and understands (like Egypt) that the road to Washington leads through Jerusalem. It certainly wants the Golan [Heights] back, but the most important relationship it wants to have is with the United States. So the United States needs to be the sponsor, and ultimately the underwriter, of such an agreement. But

Turkey can still have a role. That role needs to be tied to a more evenhanded Turkish policy in the Middle East. You cannot try to support Hamas in Gaza and mediate between Israel and Syria at the same time. That doesn't work. So that is a second element.

The third element is to look for the tensions that are built into the coalition that I have described. One of them has been mentioned twice before. There is a latent tension, and there is a potential clash between Iran and Turkey. Ultimately, both of these countries want to be hegemonic. They don't have identical interests; sometimes they have divergent interests. Presently, they seem to collaborate, but that need not be the case for good, and that is something that creative diplomacy (Israeli, but not only Israeli) can work on.

Second, Iran and Syria also do not necessarily have identical interests. In Lebanon right now, they collaborate. If you look at the issue of the international tribunal, both Iran and Hezbollah in Syria worked to undermine the tribunal and exert joint pressure on the government of Mr. [Saad] Hariri. But look five or ten years down the road. If present trends continue and Hezbollah becomes dominant in Lebanon, it will run against the ambition of Syria to hold sway in Lebanon. The Syrians know that and understand that, but they need more diplomatic tools to work on that. That is an issue that can be explored and exploited. So that definitely is another possibility.

Something else that Israeli foreign policy and diplomacy has been doing recently is to look for another periphery; that is to say, go behind Turkey and look for allies. If Turkey is becoming less friendly or hostile, then of course the immediate choice is Greece. There has been a major rapprochement in Israeli–Greek relations in recent months. Of course historically, in the 1950s and 1960s, definitely that was not the case, but it is very much the case now.

So to wrap up, recent developments in the Middle East have transformed the regional arena. From an Israeli point of view, on the whole, these have been negative, not positive elements. But there is room for diplomacy. The most important is reviving the peace process, making it work, and laying the groundwork for a new set of relationships and reinforcing the moderate elements in the Middle East, but also taking other opportunities inside the region and on the region's rims.

CHAPTER FOURTEEN

THE ARAB DIMENSION OF THE REGIONAL SYSTEM

SHIBLEY TELHAMI

I would like to make four broad points about the Arab dimension of the regional system. I'll talk about it both at the level of the public and public opinion and at the level of governments and the strategic calculations as I see them today. Let me start with the huge gap between government positions and public opinion on major strategic issues of the day. That is quite obvious on the Arab–Israeli issue, on the Iran issue, on the Turkey issue, and on the U.S. issue.

Let me start with the obvious. For Arab states, particularly those in the Gulf region, whether it is Saudi Arabia, Qatar, the United Arab Emirates, Kuwait, Oman, or any of the Gulf states, and certainly for Egypt, Jordan, and Morocco, the U.S. is an indispensable ally and, in some instances, really a state that helps them achieve their security, particularly after the decline of Iraqi power.

If you look at Arab public opinion in the six states in which I poll with Zogby International—Egypt, Saudi Arabia, Morocco, Lebanon, the United Arab Emirates [UAE], and Jordan—when you ask people, "Name the two countries that are most threatening to you personally," roughly 90 percent pretty much year after year identify Israel first, and roughly 80 percent identify the United States second. Roughly about 10 percent identify Iran third. So when you look at the priorities of public perception of how they view the threats, particularly the choices that the U.S. is putting on the table, that is different from the calculations of most Arab governments.[1]

---

1 Shibley Telhami, principle investigator, "2010 Arab Public Opinion Poll," conducted by the University of Maryland in conjunction with Zogby International (Washington, DC: Brookings Institution, August 5, 2010; online at http://www.brookings.edu/~/media/Files/rc/reports/2010/08_arab_opinion_poll_telhami /08_arab_opinion_poll_telhami.pdf).

That trend, by the way, varies a little bit. The Iranian threat is a little bit higher in the UAE and Saudi Arabia. But it is still in third place, and that is remarkable, including in countries that are neighboring. I think sometimes people misunderstand in some ways the sentiment on Iran. It is not that there is a love for Iran in the Arab world. It is clear that Iran is seen in the Arab world as the "enemy of my enemy," and when there is anger with Israel and the United States, there is more sympathy for Iran. So this year, for example, in the polling for the first time a slight majority of those we polled in the six countries think the Middle East would actually be a better place if Iran were to acquire nuclear weapons. That is quite a dramatic position to take given where the governments' positions are.

This also is reflected in the worldview that the Arab public has. When you ask them in an open question, "Name the leader that you admire most in the world; name who-ever you want, outside your own country" (I don't put them in a position to choose their own leaders), invariably, since we started doing this, almost a decade, sitting Arab leaders are not among the heroes. Typically, this year the number-one leader who is most admired is the prime minister of Turkey [Recep Tayyip Erdoğan]. The number-two leader who is admired is Hugo Chávez [of Venezuela]. The number-three leader who is admired is the leader of Hezbollah, Hassan Nasrallah. The number-four leader who is admired is Mahmoud Ahmadinejad of Iran. These, by the way, don't get huge numbers. The top vote-getter gets about 20 percent; they can name anyone they want in the world. But still, if you look at the ranking, it gives you the mind-set. It is exactly the opposite of the leaders who would be selected by Arab governments.

So when we say, "Arabs want to join in a coalition against Iran," or "Arabs want to see war in Iran," first of all, keep in mind that people are talking about governments. They are not talking about the public, because the public is of different minds. Yes, it varies from country to country, but not as much as you might think. By and large, this is the public sentiment.

Second, on the public level, there is no avoiding the fact that the Arab public looks at the world—including at Iran and Turkey, including at Latin America, including at the United States, including at the rest of the world—through the prism of the Arab–Israeli issue. If you look at the polling that we have, every single question that we ask—including the "heroes" that I just put on the table—are heroes not because people embrace them or even in some cases know a lot about them (like in the case of Hugo Chavez), but they know that they have taken a position that they like on the Arab–Israeli issue. This is the judgment that they have passed throughout the past decade. Iraq matters too, by the way, and I'll come back to that.

We see it also in the poll this year in terms of attitudes toward President Barack Obama. I know we had this theory last year that it's all about attitudes toward "the Muslim world." Let's change the rhetoric and be nice to the Muslim world, and yes, the Cairo speech transformed reality.[2] I think that was an inaccurate understanding of where the Arab public is. One way to understand how this was a misconception is to understand that even before the Cairo speech, in the poll we conducted in April and May 2009, you had a plurality of Arabs for the first time having a favorable view of the American president and only a small minority having a negative view.[3] We found nothing like it in previous years. More than 50 percent were then optimistic about American policy in the Middle East, before the Cairo speech. The speech may have helped a little bit, but this was not the basis of the shift that had taken place before.

This year when we polled among the same publics, we found that the overwhelming majority has an unfavorable view of President Obama. Those who have a favorable view of the president are less than 20 percent. The overwhelming majority of Arabs are pessimistic about American policy in the Middle East. When you ask them, "Why are you passing that judgment?"—especially given what the president said about Islam

2 Office of the White House Press Secretary, "Remarks by the President on a New Beginning," Cairo University, Cairo, Egypt, June 4, 2009, http://www.whitehouse.gov/the-press-office/remarks-president-cairo-university-6-04-09.

3 Telhami presented data from the April–May 2009 polling that both included and excluded Egypt from the sample. With Egypt, Obama was viewed very positively by 11 percent, somewhat positively by 34 percent, and neutrally by 28 percent. Without Egypt, the then-new American president registered 14 percent very positive, 46 percent somewhat positive, and 13 percent neutral. Shibley Telhami, principle investigator, "2009 Annual Arab Public Opinion Survey," conducted by the University of Maryland in conjunction with Zogby International (Washington, DC: Brookings Institution, May 19, 2009; online at http://www.brookings.edu/~/media/Files/events/2009/0519_arab_opinion/2009_arab_public_opinion_poll.pdf?bcsi_scan_A3B57DF156DD50F8=0&bcsi_scan_filename=2009_arab_public_opinion_poll.pdf).

and Muslims in the Cairo speech—they do say that of all the policies in the past year of the Obama administration toward the Middle East, they like his new attitudes toward the Muslim world the most. They acknowledge that. But when you ask them, "What explains the change of views about the administration," 61 percent say the Arab–Israeli issue, and another 30 percent say the Iraq War. Very few people, by the way, say democracy, or economic aid, or any of that sort. Basically, those are the issues that they identify.

Over and over again, we find that people pass judgment through this prism, the prism of the Arab–Israeli issue. That was certainly true, and I think was a misunderstanding about the Cairo speech as well. People thought maybe there was something about people accepting who the president was, or expecting more about him personally. We don't find any evidence of that. It was that they heard a different rhetoric from him when he came to office, particularly his being prepared to pull out of Iraq and high-lighting the Arab–Israeli peacemaking, and they were hopeful about those two issues more than any other. Their expectations were high—and they were raised by the Cairo speech, no doubt—and when, in their view, the administration didn't deliver, attitudes changed dramatically.

It is true that Arab governments still today have the capacity to ignore public opinion. They have done that over the decades, and they've done it as recently as over the Iraq War, the Gaza war, and the Lebanon war. In many ways, you have to ask the question, why does it matter? We have been asking governments to do things that the public didn't support. In the 2003 war, 90 percent of Arabs opposed the Iraq War. Then we asked governments to support us, and they did, including hosting our bases in the region to conduct attacks on Iraqi soil. So why couldn't this happen again? I think it could. I'm a realist about that. I think Arab governments have the capacity. But let's have no illusion.

What happens when you do that? Two things. One, you force them to be even more repressive than they were before. How are you going to go against passionate public opinion on the issues that matter most and expect them to allow freedom of speech and opposition to their policies? That doesn't happen. That's why I think there has been less freedom since the Iraq War in 2003, despite what we have said or the kind of experiments that we have done, precisely because of that. Second, obviously, it pushes people to the basement. I think one of the dangers that we now have is for groups like al-Qaeda and its affiliates to take foothold in parts of the Arab world, as they have in Yemen, and whether or not they will exploit opening somewhere else. That remains to be seen.

It does come at a cost, but it's possible. Still, I also think we are not fully coming to grips with the government calculations, even separate from their attitudes toward their publics, what they can do, how they read the public, and their need to respond or not to respond to their public.

Let me talk about two dimensions. One is the differences among Arab states. When we talk about "Arab states," we talk as if there is a bloc of Arab states, but there isn't, not even on issues where we think there is unanimity, such as Iran, separate from Syria. Second, in terms of what I call an Arab elite sentiment about where the Arab world is today in relative terms, in terms of distribution of power regionally and globally.

Let me reflect very quickly on those two points. When people say Arab governments want to join in an effort to prevent Iran from acquiring nuclear weapons, including the possibility of war, I think there is an inaccuracy in the description of the Arab world. There is no question in my mind that most Arab governments do not want to see Iranian dominance in the Arab world. That, by the way, includes Syria, which does need a strategic relationship with Iran in the foreseeable future. In my view, that is primarily an instrumental strategic relationship that is connected more to the prospects of Syria getting back its territory occupied by Israel.

There is no question that Arab governments across the board worry about the rise of Iranian influence. That is accurate, I think, certainly since the decline of Iraqi power with the Iraq War. Nobody sees a rise of an Iraq that will balance Iran in any foreseeable future. So in that sense, most Arab governments, if not every Arab government, is somewhat worried about the rise of Iranian influence. But they are not worried about it in the same way, and they don't see it as the same priority. That matters a lot in policy making. Israel is worried about it for military reasons, not so much because it worries about an attack by a nuclear Iran, but about the empowering of groups that might then carry out attacks against Israel without Israel having capacity to retaliate. But even the possibility of war has to loom somewhere in the background. When Egypt worries about Iran, they don't worry about Iran attacking Egypt. Yes, Egypt wants to see a nuclear-free Middle East, and they have been backing that in a big way, and they have gotten an agreement on a summit next year to be held on a nuclear-free Middle East. But they don't worry about Iran attacking Egypt.

Jordan doesn't worry about Iran attacking Egypt; Morocco doesn't worry about Iran attacking Egypt. What they're worried about is Iranian influence. What is Iranian influence in this particular case? They worry about Iran supporting groups they oppose, including Hamas and Hezbollah. They worry about the popularity of Iran in their own political community in a way that undermines them. And they connect all of that with the prospects of Arab–Israeli peace. They think that primarily the empowerment of Iran isn't a function of Iran acquiring nuclear weapons, it is a function of the absence of Arab–Israeli peace, which plays into their hands and makes them more influential. Therefore, the focus by most of the countries outside the immediate countries in the Gulf region isn't really about a war option or a military option vis-à-vis Iran, it is more about limiting Iranian influence. That is why they see the answer to it primarily in the peacemaking realm.

That is not true, of course, of all the Arab states. I think some of the smaller Arab states along the Gulf do worry about Iran in a profoundly military way, including and especially the United Arab Emirates. They have territories they claim they own that Iran controls. I think that is likely to continue. So they are not all of the same mind. We have to keep that in mind. We can't lump them together.

I would say the bulk of the Arab states outside the immediate Gulf region worry about Iran more in terms of political influence. Yes, the nuclear issue is bigger in some ways because it could fuel some competition, put pressure on them psychologically, but they are not worried about Iran attacking them.

The third point I want to make, which will be the final point, is that beyond the calculations of each Arab state and the differences among them on strategic issues, there is a pervasive, even elite sentiment—I don't want to just say the public sentiment, that's clear—but even governments themselves and the elites around them, across most of the region, there is a sense along the lines that Itamar [Rabinovich] brought up: that the relative power of the Arab world has diminished. Certainly since the end of the Cold War and certainly since the Iraq War, with the decline of Iraq, primarily because it has empowered Iran. And Turkey now has an opening to play a greater role in the Middle East. It began with the end of the Cold War and maybe with the European inaction on admitting Turkey to the European Union, but certainly the decline of Iraq opened that even more. So there is no question that even Arab elites feel that the relative clout of Arab states has diminished, to the benefit of non-Arab states (Israel, Turkey, and Iran).

In some ways you can see that in the internal debates among elites in various places. One of the most interesting cases is the case of Egypt. In my own view, Egypt has been the anchor of the political order that we have had, certainly since the Camp David Accords were signed with Israel [in 1978]. It has been an anchor of the American policy in some ways in the Middle East, certainly around the Egyptian–Israeli peace treaty.

Egypt has been the Arab leader for decades, and in some ways, I argued in a book I wrote about the Camp David Accords,[4] it was the relative decline of Egypt in economic terms in the 1960s and 1970s (to the benefit of the oil states) that has pushed Egypt to readjust its foreign policy in a way that Egypt thought would give it more clout than it was having by the late 1970s. And in fact, Egypt has been able to regain a lot of clout, primarily putting itself forth as an interlocutor between Israel and the Arabs on the one hand, between the U.S. and other Arab actors on the other. That influence, Egyptian-projected ability to help bring Arab–Israeli peace, propelled Egypt to see a benefit from this relationship that emerged out of Camp David, even separate from the economic and military support it was receiving from the United States.

I think there is a sense in Egypt that the benefits are not clear anymore. Economically, they are not the dominant power in the Arab world. The military is not used in any leveraged way vis-à-vis any part of the region. The media that Egypt controlled very much in the 1950s and 1960s no longer is dominated by Egypt, and Egypt is no longer really the key player in the relationship between the U.S. and the Arab world.

Nevertheless, it has a central role still, and I think Egypt is still the anchor in some ways of what might happen in the Arab world. You can see that even those critics of Egypt—we see today attacks against Egypt, particularly emanating from the Syrian press, about its role—even those who criticize Egypt, in effect they are admitting how central Egypt is. What they are saying in essence is that if Egypt does this, then we would be in a different place. They are acknowledging that Egypt has a role to play.

My own view is that Egyptian elites are at a point of really reassessing where they need to go. It is not likely to happen anytime soon. They are pretty committed to the peace with Israel, they are committed to the relationship with the U.S. But if we go through a political transition anytime soon, as is expected—whether it is going to be two years or five years—I think there are going to be far-reaching ramifications for the Arab political order, and therefore for the regional political order.

---

4 Shibley Telhami, *Power and Leadership in International Bargaining: The Path to the Camp David Accords* (New York: Columbia University Press, 1990).

CHAPTER FIFTEEN

DISCUSSION OF SHIFTING REGIONAL DYNAMICS

MODERATED BY GENEIVE ABDO

uestion: I have a question for Ambassador Rabinovich. I very much agree with and admire your statement of the position on both Israel–Palestine and Israel–Syria. I wonder if you could give an appraisal of what you see of the prospects internally within Israel of that viewpoint prevailing in the near term.

Itamar Rabinovich: Thank you. Since some of my co-panelists have mentioned the difference between government and society, decision making and public opinion, Israeli public opinion in this regard is an interesting case. If you were to poll the Israeli public today, as people do, and ask them about withdrawal from 94 percent of the West Bank, and a land swap, and withdrawal from the Golan Heights in return for a core peace with Syria, probably 70 percent would be against it. If a government manages to negotiate either agreement within these contours and presents the public with a done deal, it would get 70 percent in a referendum or it would win an election if it were to run in an election in order to ratify or get support for these agreements.

Right now, we have a right-wing government struggling with these issues. We have a public that in referenda or public opinion polls votes 70 percent against. Nor do we have simple partners to negotiate with: Palestinian politics is complex, it is a divided polity. Syria says that it wants to make peace, but it wants to keep all options open, including the relationship with Iran and Hezbollah. The U.S. sponsor has been pre-occupied until a couple of days ago,[1] so it was not a good time for the peace process.

---

1 The reference is to the 2010 midterm elections in the United States, which were held on November 2.

I very much hope the [Barack H. Obama] administration will decide, with whatever calculus, that it wants to become even more active than it was in the Middle East before and move the peace process. We don't have the time to get into scenarios, but I think it is doable on both fronts.

Question: My question is specifically about Yemen. It has a multifaceted security problem. The Saudis are certainly involved, the U.S. is increasingly involved. The government has often commented that there is a sort of dark foreign hand that is involved with a Shi'ite-affiliated tribal rebellion in the north. I would be curious to know, what is Iran's plan in Yemen, and how does that fit into the larger regional strategy?

Question: My question is to Dr. Taşpınar. I would like to build on what Dr. Telhami said about Prime Minister [Recep Tayyip] Erdoğan. On the one hand, Turkey is viewed, as you described, as having the best democracy ever in its history. On the other hand, such as in freedom of press, Turkey's ranking is decreasing sharply in recent years. Also, Erdoğan is being viewed as an authoritarian leader in the world. Would you please describe how this discrepancy happens?

Second, building on Ambassador Rabinovich's point about public opinion, has the Turkish administration fit the public opinion in terms of relations with Israel or anti–U.S. sentiment, at a time when President Obama has invested so much in relations with Turkey?

Question: One more for Ambassador Rabinovich and Mr. Taşpınar. We don't hear much about the Iranian regular military forces. Is there any possibility that they, in light of the difficulties over the last election, might get an independent view on things? I know they are jealous of the Revolutionary Guards.

Rabinovich: The regular Iranian army does not preoccupy Israel in the following sense.

We don't expect that there will be a direct, conventional military clash between Iran and Israel. The most likely form of aggression, if Iran decides to exert one against Israel, would be to use the 40,000 rockets and missiles that are deposited with Hezbollah in Lebanon. That would pose a significant problem in Israel without an obvious return address. So we certainly look at the conventional forces of Iran, at the nuclear issue, the air force, and other capabilities, and they are quite impressive, but we are mostly preoccupied with the rockets that are in Lebanon and increasingly so in Gaza, and to some extent subject to a button being pushed in Tehran.

Alex Vatanka: On the issue of the regular armed forces, what the Islamic Republic has done very carefully for the last 31 years is to basically learn the lesson that the Iranian regular armed forces were a brainchild of the U.S. military, going back to the 1950s. The fact that that heritage existed, they never trusted their regular armed forces. They have never really, in the last 31 years, given them the kind of political clout where they could become a player. Certainly the regular armed forces of Iran are nowhere politically placed to be able to rival IRGC [Islamic Revolutionary Guard Corps]. Whatever they might feel about the money and resources that gets into the IRGC, they are not in a position to challenge the IGRC because they've had their wings clipped off for a long time.

On Yemen, when you refer to "dark forces," you are referring to Saudi accusations and the statements that President Abdullah Saleh himself has made, although indirectly, about Iranian involvement. As an analyst, I haven't seen the hard evidence. Whether Iran might be involved or not, that is plausible, but I can say the Iranian–Yemeni connection is weak at best. The Twelver/Jafari Shi'a and the Zaidis of Yemen really don't have much in terms of historical affinity. Certainly one could not make the comparison between the Hezbollah of Lebanon and the Iranians. The connection just does not even deserve a comparison because they are so distinct. But you can't discount that Iran might be involved.

The big question for me is whether that is state-sponsored Iranian intervention in Yemen, because that would make it much more interesting, or whether Iranian foundations, religious foundations often connected in one way or another to the state, are involved in Yemen. That has also been the accusation. The Yemenis are not just pointing the finger at Iran, they are pointing the finger at Bahraini, Saudi, and Iraqi Shi'a as well, some sort of pan-regional Shi'a effort to help their brethren in Yemen.

Shibley Telhami: The key point I was making about the popularity of the Turkish prime minister or the Iranian president is that people are seeing them primarily through the prism of the Arab–Israeli issue, and secondarily through Iraq. We saw that even in 2002–3, when in France there was the issue of the veil in schools. It was mostly Arab immigrants who were revolting and having confrontations with the police, and there was a lot of press coverage in the Arab world. In 2002, 2003, 2004, the leader who was identified as most popular in the six countries where I do polling in the Arab world was [then-French President] Jacques Chirac. It was primarily because he hosted Yasir Arafat when he was dying, and treated him like a head of state, and went to receive him, [which got] tremendous coverage. And he opposed the Iraq War at the UN [United Nations]. Those two were basically the reward things. We didn't see [Hezbollah leader] Hassan Nasrallah emerge as a popular leader in places like Egypt or Jordan or Morocco—largely Sunni Arab states—until the 2006 war [against Israel] and how he was seen to have performed in that war.

With the Turkish government, broadly—not even the prime minister—if we look at the rise of Turkey now in the Arab world, it really started with the Turkish opposition to the Iraq War. People rewarded Turkey for it for two reasons. One, because it just opposed the war, but two, as an example of a Muslim country that they thought was taking public opinion into account, unlike their own states. So that was really the opening that provided Turkey with reaching out. Then Turkey's position on Gaza—particularly during the Gaza war, since the Gaza war, the Turkish flotilla incident (and I did the polling after the Gaza flotilla incident in the summer)—all of that entailed that the public was rewarding Turkey and rewarding the prime minister for those issues.

Ömer Taşpınar: I think the illiberal tendencies in Turkish society are alive and well. Turkey is becoming more democratic, but liberal democracy is something else. It is more democratic in the sense that when you look at the way the European Union assesses Turkey's progress report, overall, the direction is not towards a more authoritarian Turkey; otherwise, Turkey would not have started accession negotiations in 2005. Overall, the direction is towards more civilian supremacy over the military and overall better freedom of expression.

However, the problem with the press that you mentioned is a real one. It reflects the power struggle in Turkey, somewhat simplistically referred to as between the secularist camp and the more pro-government camp. There is nothing excusable in a tax penalty established against a very major media group in Turkey. On the other hand, to conclude from this that Turkey is turning into an authoritarian Islamist state would be not taking into consideration the way the European Union itself and most of the other monitoring institutions look at Turkey.

So overall, the tendency is toward more democratization, but liberalism is a different question.

Question: All the speakers have referred to and named so many countries, stretching from Iran, Turkey, Persian Gulf states, Jordan, Saudi Arabia, even Morocco and Egypt, where the U.S. has tremendous leverage and influence. But the entire world is going through a transformation, and there is a transition going on from a unipolar world to a multipolar world. If that happens, what would be then the scenario and the dynamics? What level of influence and leverage would the U.S. have to influence, to bring peace and prosperity in that region? Do you think the natural course of history also has anything to do with what happens in the world?

Geneive Abdo: You're asking, to leverage U.S. power in the region? Is that what you're asking?

Question: Yes, everybody says without the mediation, facilitation, involvement, and engagement by the U.S., it is not possible to resolve such issues in the Middle East. Active engagement is a necessity and mandatory. I am saying the world is going through a transition from a unipolar to a multipolar world. In that scenario, what would be the level of influence and leverage the U.S. will have on those countries in the region to bring them to the negotiating table?

Telhami: First off, the U.S. has an overwhelming presence in the Middle East—military presence. That is both in the short term, maybe stabilizing vis-à-vis Iran, but in the long term, it is a source of discontent and certainly opposition in the Arab world. But the most important thing the U.S. can do, given what I think is going on regionally, is for the U.S. to help deliver Arab–Israeli peace. I think that is a key to unlocking the current inequality of power in the region, and that is an area that the U.S. is indispensable. I don't think Arab–Israeli peace can take place without an aggressive American role.

Vatanka: A quick summary of the Iranian position on this, and I think it's quite telling when arguably the most anti-American state in the Middle East (at least on paper) comes out and says in so many words, so often, that of course the United States is going to stay in the region. The question is, would they give us what we think we deserve as this large nation called Iran? Would they respect us? If you listen to the speeches of [President Mahmoud] Ahmadinejad and others, Supreme Leader [Ali] Khamenei, even the Iranians appreciate that the U.S. is not going to go anywhere.

By the way, who is going to replace the U.S.? The Iranians have just again burned their fingers in terms of relations with the Russians. The Chinese are not going to come in. So there isn't really an alternative to the U.S. staying as part of the security arrangements of this region.

Rabinovich: I agree with both my predecessors, but I would say this. In the aftermath of two unsuccessful wars in the Middle East, and given the economic prospects in this country, in relative terms, I see a decline in U.S. influence.

Taşpınar: From the perspective of Ankara, the last 20 years of American foreign policy toward the Middle East has been largely a failure. So overall, this tendency that the U.S. has to be there for things to go better is not really shared in the mind-set of the current Turkish government and, most importantly, public opinion. Hence the new sense of Turkish independence, the new sense that Turkey should pursue its own national interest and should not be obligated all the time to follow what comes from Washington.

Villagers in Baghvanay, Nangarhar Province, Afghanistan, on May 21, 2009, during a humanitarian assistance operation in the area by the Afghan National Army,
supported by Embedded Training Team 7-4. (LtCol David A. Benhoff, USMCR)

PART FOUR

REEVALUATING U.S. POLICY IN AFGHANISTAN AND PAKISTAN

CHAPTER SIXTEEN

AFGHANISTAN AND PAKISTAN—
WHERE ARE WE?

BRIAN KATULIS

I want to talk about three main things. One, where are we, heading into the December [2010] review, both in Afghanistan and Pakistan?[1] I'm sure the other panelists will fill in and dispute certain issues or will agree. Second, I'll highlight what I think is a very weak link in the Afghanistan component of our strategy. Third, I'll talk about some challenges ahead in Pakistan.

First, where are we? I think it is important to look at this particular phase—call it a "surge," call it what you will—as a phase of intensified resources. If you want to divide the present and the period that started with 9/11 into three phases and where I think we're heading, I think you can talk about three distinct phases. From 2002 to 2008, in both Afghanistan and Pakistan, we had a period of not-so-benign neglect, where much of our resources, attention, and time were diverted by the war in Iraq. You can see the effect of this in Afghanistan, of leaving the mission unaccomplished: the steady growth of the Taliban insurgency since 2005. You see also in Pakistan what Ahmed Rashid called the "descent into chaos,"[2] but a lot of what was happening—and I know Hassan [Abbas] is going to talk in greater detail about this—but that first phase from 2002 to 2008 was one in which toward the end of it our Chairman of the Joint Chiefs of Staff told Congress that in Afghanistan we do what we can, in Iraq we do what we must.[3]

---

1 Office of the White House Press Secretary, "Overview of the Afghanistan and Pakistan Annual Review," December 16, 2010, http://www.whitehouse.gov/the-press-office/2010/12/16/overview-afghanistan-and-pakistan-annual-review.

2 Ahmed Rashid, *Descent into Chaos: The United States and the Failure of Nation Building in Pakistan, Afghanistan, and Central Asia* (New York: Viking, 2008).

3 Admiral Michael G. Mullen, chairman of the Joint Chiefs of Staff, testified before the House Armed Services Committee on December 11, 2007, that "in Afghanistan, we do what we can. In Iraq, we do what we must." (http://crs.gov/Pages/Reports.aspx?ProdCode=RL33110).

If you look at 2009 essentially until 2011, it is a period of intensified resources and attention, not only on the part of the U.S., but of NATO [North Atlantic Treaty Organization] allies, not only in terms of troops, but much more money and development assistance, and more political efforts. Similarly, across the border in Pakistan, you have an intensified effort on the U.S. side through strategic dialogue, ongoing consultations with security officials, and much more time devoted to Pakistan and helping its government deal with its issues.

So we are in the second phase; we are just past the midterm period in this 2009–11 period. It is a bit unclear in terms of progress or steps backward. And I think the second phase is preparing us for what will be the third phase, which I think will be discussed much more at Lisbon: the preparation for a gradual transfer of authority in Afghanistan from 2011 to 2014. I know everyone has been fixated on the summer 2011 timeline, but I think the discussions at Lisbon next week will further reaffirm that the full transfer of authority in Afghanistan is not likely to happen until 2014. I think there is even some question along those lines.[4]

So where are we? The picture is not very clear, and the results are mixed, for a number of reasons. In Afghanistan, the conflict is quite complicated, and it belies the broad categories that framed our public debate last fall, when the [Barack H.] Obama administration was debating different options. The counterterrorism (CT) vs. counterinsurgency (COIN) models left the impression that there was some sort of unified national strategy that we were looking at. If you look at what actually has happened over the last year and a half, we have different military strategies, different overall strategies, in different parts of the country. There has been more or less a full-scale COIN effort in the southern part of the country in Helmand [Province] and Kandahar, which has more or less the prescribed troop-to-population ratio in place. Kandahar seems to be going

4 NATO held a summit in Lisbon, Portugal, on November 18–20, 2010, that included representatives of the 28 NATO allies, 20 partner countries that have contributed forces to the efforts in Afghanistan, and Afghan President Hamid Karzai. As Katulis predicted, NATO and Afghanistan agreed on a phased transfer of authority and security responsibility that will be scheduled for completion by the end of 2014, with supporting troops from the NATO alliance expected to remain well beyond that date. Steven Erlanger and Jackie Calmes, "NATO Sees Long-Term Role after Afghan Combat," *New York Times*, November 21, 2010, http://www.nytimes.com/2010/11/21/world/europe/21nato.html?_r=1&scp=5&sq=NATO%20Afghanistan%20Lisbon&st=cse. See also NATO coverage of the summit (http://www.nato.int/cps/en/SID-0F77ABC8-62AA585C/natolive/news_68877.htm).

a little bit better from a security standpoint than other places, like Marjah, and we apparently have had some success against some of the Taliban from a security standpoint.

In the eastern part of the country, and I think this is one feature that comes up in our news here and there—there was a very good *Army Times* article earlier this fall about this[5]—there has been an intensified effort by the Joint Special Operations Command against the various networks here. This may be closer to the CT model, and in fact there is a focused effort particularly on the Haqqani network there. In the north and west, we have in Kunduz, Mazar-e Sharif, and Herat what I think ISAF [International Security Assistance Force] and others have labeled economy-of-force operations. There have been mixed results there, and in fact some possible gains from the Taliban.

So if you just read the newspaper headlines from the last week of October, we are in a confusing period. The *New York Times* on October 20: "Coalition Forces Routing Taliban in Key Afghan Region." Three days later, the *Washington Post*: "General Petraeus Says Progress is Faster Than Expected in Afghanistan Operations." Four days later, the *Washington Post* again: "U.S. Military Campaign to Topple Resilient Taliban Hasn't Succeeded."[6]

So we are in this phase where, again, we have applied more resources, and clearly it is having some sort of impact. Gathering the data and assessing where we're at is a very difficult task, for two main reasons. One, it is a complicated conflict in Afghanistan. Two, I think there is an imperative on the part of some parts of some U.S. agencies to try to present progress as part of the overall effort to either set the table for some sort of negotiation there, or to impact public opinion back at home.

---

5 Sean D. Naylor, "JSOC Task Force Battles Haqqani Militants," *Army Times*, September 13, 2010, http://www.armytimes.com/news/2010/09/army-haqqani-092010w/.

6 Carlotta Gall, "Coalition Forces Routing Taliban in Key Afghan Region," *New York Times*, October 20, 2010, http://www.nytimes.com/2010/10/21/world/asia/21kandahar.html; Rajiv Chandrasekaran and Joshua Partlow, "Gen. Petraeus Says Progress is Faster than Expected in Afghanistan Operation," *Washington Post*, October 23, 2010, http://www.washingtonpost.com/wp-dyn/content/article/2010/10/22 /AR20101 02204 609.html; Greg Miller, "U.S. Military Campaign to Topple Resilient Taliban Hasn't Succeeded," *Washington Post*, October 27, 2010, http://www.washingtonpost.com/wp-dyn/content /article/2010/10/26/ AR2010102606571.html.

But to sum up, in Afghanistan, I think overall we seem to be in a period where there is some impact, obviously when you put the finest military force on the ground in some places, but it is uncertain whether this is actually adding up to anything that will be sustainable in the long run. Special operations forces seem to be doing well, defined in terms of their narrow category or lane, but does this add up to sustainable security? That remains an open question. There has been some progress in training the security forces in Afghanistan, some steps toward achieving that goal. As we know from Iraq, it is the surge of local forces that matters a lot more than the enabling presence that foreign troops have. Some of the other issues, in terms of reconciliation, we have had some talk towards that, but it remains an open question since there seems to be little political movement from President [Hamid] Karzai on some of the internal reforms.

All of this paints a very mixed picture. There is a separate question, which I think Paul [Pillar] will address: what does this mean for U.S. national security interests? Do we have a balanced portfolio?

I want to highlight two other points. One is what I think is one of the weakest links in Afghanistan right now: the political and development components of our strategy. It is a component that the U.S. and our international partners are responsible for, and it also requires responsibility on the part of the Afghan government. We have seen this in several places. A big problem is that the Afghan government does not appear to be showing up on the civilian side, even when we have seen some success in clearing operations. We can do some of the building ourselves, but it can't hold forever without some sort of Afghan government filling in these spots. We see this in Kandahar. It was highlighted prominently that nearly two-thirds of the city's government positions remain unfilled despite some strong incentives. There are some human capacity problems here. There is the threat of assassination and intimidation, which has been going on for a long time. But the civilian side of this is a big weakness and a big concern. Again, we can put our military in certain places and it can have an impact, but whether it will actually hold and allow for building a sustainable security architecture is a very real and outstanding question.

It is not only a problem on the part of the Afghan government; it is a problem in the U.S. government, too. For all of our talk about "smart power" and shifting resources to the State Department and USAID [United States Agency for International Development], agencies that have suffered from a lack of resources for decades, you need only look at the latest report by the Special Inspector General for Afghanistan Reconstruction [SIGAR], out on October 30.[7] We have spent more than $50 billion just in terms of U.S. taxpayer money in development in Afghanistan. When I travel to the country, it is hard to see what we have gotten for that $50 billion.

If you look specifically at an example of Nangarhar Province, where SIGAR did an assessment, their assessment captures a lot of what we hear from briefings we get from the U.S. government. A hundred million dollars of assistance, yet we have no operational development plan. USAID-funded projects are implemented without the knowledge or cooperation of national or local government authorities. Of the operational budget in this one province, 4 percent of it goes actually to development, and 85 percent of it goes to salaries and overhead.

Again, for all of the talk—and I think we have been supportive of it; I wrote a book on this in 2008 about the need to rebalance our national security portfolio[8]—for all of the good talk about smart power, Afghanistan is one of the ultimate tests of this. I think at this phase, we are failing it, for a number of different reasons, in part because of our lack of focus on the capacity of the civilian side of the government. There are other issues, too, in terms of absorptive capacity on the part of our Afghan partners. We have received, and Caroline [Wadhams] has been in some of these briefings from NGO [nongovernmental organization] and development professionals who say, "You are simply flooding the country with cash that it can't absorb." It is actually creating greater dys-

---

7 Special Inspector General for Afghanistan Reconstruction, "Quarterly Report to the United States Congress, October 30, 2010" (http://www.sigar.mil/pdf/quarterlyreports/Oct2010/Lores /SIGAR 4Q_ 2010Book.pdf). All of the SIGAR reports can be accessed online (http://www.sigar.mil/ReportToCo ngress.asp).

8 Nancy E. Soderberg and Brian Katulis, *The Prosperity Agenda: What the World Wants from America—and What We Need in Return* (Hoboken, NJ: John Wiley & Sons, 2008).

function rather than stability. So this is one of the weakest links. We can build Afghan security forces. That will be a much harder process than what we did in Iraq. But the weakest link is the civilian side.

A last comment on Pakistan. We have had an effort, which I have supported, to move beyond a transactional relationship with Pakistan. This was at the heart of the funding assistance through Kerry-Lugar,[9] a lot of the ideas that were discussed in 2006–7. Though we have seen some steps forward in terms of activity, intensified efforts by the State Department and others, when you measure what's happening in Pakistan, I think it's still a very mixed result. It is in part the fault of our Pakistani partners, and in part our fault, too, in terms of how we do business.

In essence, one of the key problems that we are facing is that the Pakistani security establishment still controls much of Pakistan's security and foreign policy. I think it is still an open question as to whether their calculations have changed. I know General [David H.] Petraeus was in Islamabad yesterday talking yet again about the need for activity and operations in North Waziristan, but I don't know that we've seen a fundamental shift on the Pakistani side. I know Hassan is going to talk a lot about this. But for all the talk about a new strategic partnership and the need to move beyond transactional deals, it seems like much of the focus—despite the efforts in the strategic dialogue, despite the additional development assistance—remains stuck in the past. We need to continue to work at it. The additional challenge of the disaster assistance with the flood,[10] and the reprogramming of the money, creates another impediment, but we need to continue to work at it. Pakistan, in my view, is at the crux and heart of many of the regional security challenges.

---

9 Commonly known by the name of its most prominent sponsors, Senators John F. Kerry and Richard G. Lugar and Congressman Howard L. Berman, the *Enhanced Partnership with Pakistan Act of 2009* provides $1.5 billion per year in aid to Pakistan for the years 2010 through 2014. However, a U.S. Government Accountability Office report found that the U.S. only disbursed $179.5 million in the 2010 fiscal year. *Enhanced Partnership with Pakistan Act of 2009*, Public Law 111-73, 111th Cong., 1st sess., October 15, 2009, http://www.gpo.gov/fdsys/pkg/BILLS-111s1707enr/pdf/BILLS-111s1707enr.pdf; U.S. Government Accountability Office, "Department of State's Report to Congress and U.S. Oversight of Civilian Assistance to Pakistan Can Be Further Enhanced," February 27, 2011, http://www.gao.gov/new.items /d11310r.pdf.

10 For an overview of relief efforts in response to the 2010 flooding, see Kenneth H. Williams, ed., "The International Response to the 2010 Pakistan Flood: An Interview with Michael Young of the International Rescue Committee," *Marine Corps University Journal 2* (Spring 2011): 81–99.

To sum up, it's a mixed picture. We are more than halfway through what we call the surge, and I think that is mostly focused on the military side, but we need to look at the broader set of resources that can be brought to bear.

Just four concluding thoughts in terms of where I think we are heading in the next phase, this transitional phase in Afghanistan, a phase where I think we are going to need much more intensified efforts in Pakistan.

Number one, if the last two or three years have been about a recalibration or realignment from Iraq to Afghanistan and Pakistan, I think we are going to see much more focus in the next two to three years on Pakistan. By that I don't mean boots on the ground, I don't mean military invasion. What I mean is actually helping the Pakistanis wrestle with some vast development and security challenges. In some ways, it is much more difficult, from a diplomatic standpoint, to deal with, but it is essential to bring security to that part of the world.

Second, I mentioned briefly reconciliation and the peace talks in Afghanistan. It seems there is a movement afoot to look more at this as an option. There are divided views, as we hear [Central Intelligence Agency Director] Leon Panetta recently saying that he doesn't see any evidence at all that there is a seriousness of purpose on the part of members of the Taliban insurgency. [There are] people in NATO saying something different. My presumption here is that, first, reconciliation and peace talks will be an essential part of bringing peace and stability to Afghanistan. My second assumption is this is all easier said than done. This will take years, because we are not just talking about a conflict of the past eight or nine years, we are talking about a 30-year conflict that reaches beyond Afghanistan's borders.

This leads to my third concluding remark. Another weak link in the U.S. strategy is the absence of a true regional strategy. You can go on the State Department's website and take a look at what they call their regional strategy for Afghanistan and Pakistan.[11]

---

11 U.S. Department of State, "Afghanistan and Pakistan Regional Stabilization Strategy," updated February 24, 2010, http://www.state.gov/documents/organization/135728.pdf.

I think it is a good document, but it gets into the nuts and bolts of both Afghanistan and Pakistan, a lot of nation building, even though the cover note from Secretary [Hillary Rodham] Clinton says we are not nation building over there. But [the paper includes] a lot in terms of economic development and governance. What is missing is the sense of how do you use statecraft, how do you actually look at the strategic calculations of actors like India and Iran (and others neighboring Afghanistan) that have a serious stake in what is going on?

Candidate Obama talked a lot about the regional approach. What we have seen so far in the actions of the U.S. government is the absence of the use of statecraft. I know we have some friends and former colleagues in the U.S. government who are working hard on these issues of trying to get more people as part of the civilian surge in Afghanistan. I think we have gone down into the weeds and we have forgotten one key component: how do we actually, diplomatically, work the regional issues and take into account, for instance, Iran's role, which will be enduring, in Afghanistan? How do we deal with India? I know the president is going to deal with a bit of this on his trip, but I think we have dealt with it piecemeal.[12]

The last comment I would make, in closing, and it is threaded through a lot of my remarks, is that we are at this difficult phase where it is hard to assess what impact we are having. It's mixed results. But the one weakest link, and I think it's one that our generation is going to face, is actually getting serious about this smart-power business, of actually looking at the fact that for a long while, our friends in the Pentagon have had a lot of the tools to implement the policy in this part of the world, and they have done an admirable job, but as we all see, it is incomplete. When we look at trying to help societies stabilize themselves and stabilize communities, when we look at what I call the ultimate test of smart power—Afghanistan and Pakistan—and continuing the mission in Iraq, we actually have serious institutional capacity problems on our side. I am fearful of where we are going in this country in terms of our attention to these sorts of

---

12 President Obama traveled to South and East Asia soon after the 2010 midterm elections, departing on November 4 and returning to Washington on November 11. He visited India, Indonesia, South Korea, and Japan and attended the G-20 summit in Seoul. White House Schedule, November 2010, http://www.whitehouse.gov/schedule/complete/2010-W45; http://www.whitehouse.gov/schedule/complete/2010-W46.

challenges. Where I see a need to increase resources on that side to supplement the military effort—a military effort that I think will necessarily have to fade to the background—we need to continue to have an enduring presence both in Afghanistan and Pakistan on the civilian side. The way we have handled those issues in this intensified period so far leads me to be pessimistic about the possibility of achieving tangible results.

CHAPTER SEVENTEEN

MILITARY STRATEGY IN THE AFGHANISTAN–PAKISTAN THEATER

STEPHEN D. BIDDLE

I was asked to look at the military strategy in the theater. One of the things that I think is most interesting about the [General Stanley A.] McChrystal military assessment of the situation in Afghanistan is that perhaps uniquely for a military strategic assessment document, it cites as coequally necessary for success in this theater not just the improvement in security conditions—a classical, traditional military mission—but also the reform of governance in Afghanistan. McChrystal's report argued quite explicitly that if we failed to do correctly either the security side of the mission or the governance side of the mission, we would suffer defeat. To my knowledge, this is the only such military strategic assessment I'm aware of that puts that kind of emphasis on governance and that accepts it as a military responsibility and not simply something that can be handed off to or coordinated with or done in conjunction with State Department civilians, nongovernmental organizations, or the UN [United Nations].[1]

For reasons I'm going to return to in a few minutes, there is actually a very important role for military resources, military instruments, and military activity in the reform of governance in Afghanistan. Our strategy in this theater, certainly since General McChrystal took command, has explicitly recognized this.

---

1 Biddle was part of a team of experts who participated in a review of the Afghanistan strategy during the summer of 2009. General McChrystal submitted his commander's initial assessment, which was based on the efforts of this working group, to Secretary of State Robert M. Gates on August 30, 2009. The *Washington Post* published a story based on a leaked copy of the assessment on September 21, 2009; the Department of Defense declassified a lightly redacted version of the report that same day (http://media.washingtonpost.com/wp-srv/politics/documents/Assessment_Redacted_092109.pdf).

That having been said, the campaign plan that is directing our activities in this theater is much better developed in terms of implementing guidance for the actual activities of the resources we have in theater on the security side of the campaign than it is on the governance side of the campaign. For the security side, there are nested instructions of instructions of instructions going from the theater level down to the battalion and company level for all major parts of the theater. On the governance side, there is a preamble that talks about the importance of this activity, and then almost nothing on what exactly to do about it.

In the presence of that kind of situation in which the military in the theater have been told this is very important, but they haven't been given a great deal of specific guidance on what exactly to do about it as a result, what military organizations tend to do is revert to doctrine. They revert to the published written instructions for the conduct of this kind of campaign that they have all been trained in and familiarized with before they got to theater. Regrettably, U.S. military counterinsurgency doctrine at the moment has provisions for governance reform in it that are directly unhelpful with respect to the conduct of, I would argue, counterinsurgency in general, frankly, but certainly Afghanistan in particular.[2]

The central thrust of the governance dimension of current U.S. military doctrine is capacity building. The mission of the military in counterinsurgency is to provide, for host governments that don't have it, a larger force of trained civil servants and public administrators who know how to keep the sewers operating, how to collect the trash, how to keep the electricity up and running, who know how to run a spreadsheet, can do charts and all the other instrumentaria of the modern public administration profession. This is not the central problem in Afghanistan. Heaven knows there is certainly a shortage of trained, capable public administrators in Afghanistan, either in the country at large or in particularly threatened locations like Helmand or Kandahar. That is not, however, the biggest problem associated with governance in Afghanistan.

---

2 The prevailing doctrine is spelled out in U.S. Army (FM 3-24) and U.S. Marine Corps (MCWP 3-33.5), *Counterinsurgency* (Washington, DC: Department of the Army and Marine Corps Combat Development Command, 2006). This document is more widely available as U.S. Army and Marine Corps, *The U.S. Army/Marine Corps Counterinsurgency Field Manual* (Chicago: University of Chicago Press, 2007).

The biggest problem is not that a government that seeks legitimacy lacks the where-withal it needs to realize its benign intentions; the problem is that significant elements of the government in Afghanistan have malign intentions. There is a significant interest divergence between the United States and the international community and significant elements of the Afghan government. In a situation in which significant elements of the government are actively predatory on the society they govern, improving their capacity makes them more efficient predators. It does not in fact align the hearts and minds of the Afghan population with their government and our activity. At worst, it makes things worse; at best, it is beside the point. Either way, it is not what we require.

What we require, it seems to me, if we are actually going to address the real problem of governance reform in Afghanistan—which, as the McChrystal report suggested, is indeed essential for success in the undertaking—is to reconceptualize the problem of governance reform not as capacity building, but as dealing with the activities of a collection of (some have estimated) perhaps as many as a dozen networks of malign actors which function as old-fashioned patronage political machines, designed to extract resources from the society and other actors in the country and direct them upward to those higher in the pyramid in this hierarchically organized network of corrupt actors. In the process, they substantially disadvantage and existentially threaten the livelihoods of Afghan civilians who are not part of the network. If you are an Afghan civilian living in a part of the country dominated by a malign actor network of this kind—one might take as an illustrative example the problem in Kandahar Province, which is by no means the only such network in Afghanistan but is the one that has been getting the most recent public attention—you have a reasonable basis to believe that if you are going to remain outside the patronage network that is governing most official activity in the province of Kandahar, sooner or later this network, when it gets around to it, is going to take everything you own.

This is not a problem of being shaken down for petty checkpoint thievery at police depots. It is not a problem of paying a bit of *baksheesh* in order to get a driver's license. This is a problem of systematic misappropriation of public resources to the use of individuals within the network, especially but not limited to land. In an agrarian society in which land is the basis not just of wealth, but also of the basic livelihood and the wherewithal to conduct daily life for the majority of the population, and in a country in which title to land is remarkably ambiguous after a long generation of civil warfare and an active attempt by a number of combatants in those civil wars to destroy the previous system of whatever legal basis there had been for the allocation of land, when a network of malign actors centrally implicated in the government itself condemns for nominally public use private farmland and then redirects it for the economic benefit of those within the network, it is telling civilians outside the operations of this network that the very basis of their livelihood—their ability to feed their families and survive until the next week—is eventually up in the air because it could potentially be taken by a group of people over which you have no control and against whom you have no recourse. Are you going to go to the court system to get adjudication of your actual right to your farm, when it has been condemned for public use? The network owns the courts. Are you going to go to the district or provincial government to get them to stand up for your rights? They are the heart of the malign actor network in the province of Kandahar. Are you going to go to the Americans and let them protect you against this? As far as most Afghans can see, we are actively complicit in this entire process because our governance doctrine has been telling us to build capacity. We have been out there trying to build up, empower, and better train and enable the very networks of malign actors within the government that are preying upon the population. The population, therefore, not unreasonably, looks at us as complicit in this.

For a member of the Afghan population outside these networks, if you believe that they are as much of a threat to you as a reasonable person might conclude, your only recourse is to the Taliban. The Taliban, alone among apparent authority and power

160

sources, offers protection to people who are on the outs and are the losers in this system. Although the Taliban are notably unpopular—I have seen no systematic evidence, either nationally or even regionally in Afghanistan, to suggest that the Afghan people in any significant number would prefer the Taliban to any kind of nonpredatory government alternative to the Taliban—but they will nevertheless go to the Taliban and offer access to society and to populated areas if they believe that their alternative to this is predation at the hands of a network that has its boot on all the major channels of power and authority in the province. If this continues, we will lose the war, regardless of how aggressively we pursue the security part of our strategy, regardless of how well it is implemented, and regardless of how many troops are tied up in doing it.

If you see the governance problem to be addressed in Afghanistan in this way, as coping with the activities of networks of malign actors within the government—not simply as creating better administrative capacity on the part of a benignly intentioned government that is trying to do the right thing but just doesn't have enough stuff to do it yet—how would you go about developing the implementing guidance to direct a more effective undertaking in this direction? In the interest of time, I'm not going to be able to go into tremendous detail. What I will do is to sketch some of the broad outlines of what I think a campaign of this kind would require.

The first order of business is, if we are going to approach this as a problem of attacking networks, we need to look at it in a way not so unlike the way we would deal with other networks that we mean to disempower. In a military context in particular, that implies there is a certain amount of shaping activity that has to take place before we undertake decisive operations. The first element of the shaping phase of dealing with malign actor networks as a threat to governance in Afghanistan is to begin with the unbelievably exciting, gripping, thrilling issue of contract reform.

I think in many ways a useful metaphor for thinking about the functioning of these kinds of networks in Afghanistan is as a political machine that is doing work for its owners. The hydraulic fluid that allows these machines to do political work for the people who run them is money. Money is what enables the patronage networks that enable the control over activity that enable the taking of public resources for private benefit. The money that constitutes the hydraulic fluid in these political machines is coming, overwhelmingly, from us. It is not centrally narcotics money, it is primarily the redirection of American contracting, and to a lesser extent contracting activities by other international agencies in Afghanistan.

The first step to make any progress in this undertaking is to shut off the intake valves at the bottom of these pyramidal machines, reduce or eliminate the flow of American money into these networks—reduce the hydraulic pressure in the machine, and as a result, reduce the ability of the machine to do work for its owners. What that does is to set up a situation in which the coercive leverage available to us to try to bring about the removal or constraint on the behavior of malign actors could conceivably be sufficient to do the job, if first, before we apply the leverage, we reduce the power of the actors, and thus their utility to the people above them in the system.

If we start instead at the top, as we have tended to do, and we try to get, for example, the president of Afghanistan to rein in his younger brother [Ahmed Wali Karzai] or make him into an ambassador to the Seychelles, say. The president of Afghanistan believes his younger brother is performing terribly important political work for him in lining up votes and in at least ostensibly creating security in, for example, Kandahar Province. The leverage we have available vis-à-vis the Karzai government wasn't enough to get him to believe that at the end of the day, the pain we were threatening is greater than the benefit he was obtaining by not giving us what we wanted and continuing to rely on his younger brother. The coercive attempt failed.

If we prepare the battlefield first by weakening the key actors, by starting at the bottom and shutting off the money, directing our coercive resources at the next echelon up in the system—those immediately weakened by the reduction in the money flow—removing them and weakening the next echelon, by working our way up the network, we have some potential to deliver leverage that is sufficient to do the job when we reach echelons near the top.

There are any number of difficulties with this, most of which I am not going to have time to talk about, but I will at least address one: time. If you see the governance problem as being creating lots of trained public administrators whom you can then parachute into places like Marjah, for example—the "governance in a box" concept—if it was going to work, that could be done fairly quickly. That isn't actually the problem, so therefore, parachuting public administrators into threatened areas didn't provide much of a solution.

If you see the problem and the solution the way I'm talking about, however, you are not going to be able to parachute a solution into place in the next weeks or months. A substantial amount of preparatory activity has to take place, and you need to work your way slowly up the network. This is a process that is going to take more time and demand more patience of a polity and a political system that has not heretofore been suggesting that they have a great deal of patience for Afghanistan. If, however, we mean to succeed in this, a degree of patience is required, not just for the security side—to provide stability in populated parts of Afghanistan, the area in which patience has been most frequently discussed—but also with respect to the governance side of the problem. The effective way of dealing with governance, it seems to me, is not as fast and will require probably as much patience as the security side will.

CHAPTER EIGHTEEN

REEVALUATING U.S. POLICY IN AFGHANISTAN AND PAKISTAN

PAUL R. PILLAR

I'm afraid I'm going to add a bit to the pessimism that you have heard from my colleagues. The subject is reevaluating U.S. policy. We have had a need for reevaluation for some time in a war that has now gone on for nine years. The administration already last year had a review, and then a re-review, culminating in the West Point speech, which resulted in a policy that was to a large extent a political compromise that included both a surge of troops and a start date for a withdrawal, a start date which is only eight months away from right now.[1]

The most important—but not the only—issue for any further review (we are going to have another one next month)[2] is the pace and length of that withdrawal that is supposed to start next July. Is it going to be minimal and just cosmetic, or is it going to be something more substantial? Some of the main issues involved here were addressed in an unofficial report by a group of people billing themselves the Afghanistan Study Group. I have been involved in that, and like other people involved, no one of us totally agrees with everything in the report. But I agree with most of the things that are in there.[3]

---

1 Office of the White House Press Secretary, "Remarks by the President in Address to the Nation on the Way Forward in Afghanistan and Pakistan," United States Military Academy, West Point, NY, December 1, 2009, http://www.whitehouse.gov/the-press-office/remarks-president-address-nation-way-forward-afghanistan-and-pakistan. President Obama authorized a "surge" of 30,000 additional troops (General Stanley A. McChrystal had asked for 40,000) but set the date "our troops will begin to come home" at 18 months from that time (July 2011).

2 Office of the White House Press Secretary, "Overview of the Afghanistan and Pakistan Annual Review," December 16, 2010, http://www.whitehouse.gov/the-press-office/2010/12/16/overview-afghanistan-and-pakistan-annual-review.

3 Afghanistan Study Group, "A New Way Forward: Rethinking U.S. Strategy in Afghanistan," August 16, 2010, http://www.afghanistanstudygroup.org/NewWayForward_report.pdf.

We need to get away from what has been a narrow focus—not on what my colleagues have talked about, but in the larger discourse about Afghanistan—a narrow focus on how is the counterinsurgency doing, although those are very important questions, for the reasons you just heard. We need instead to address the more fundamental question of why we are doing a counterinsurgency at all in Afghanistan and whether the costs of continuing on the current course are worth whatever benefit the U.S. is receiving. I dare say much of the public discourse out there has simply lost sight of that.

The counterinsurgency, with the goals of defeating the Afghan Taliban and stabilizing Afghanistan, has come to be treated as a kind of end in itself. It is not an end in itself; it is a means. To put it in the bluntest terms, it is the result of a nine-year-long mission creep that has accompanied a deterioration of security conditions in Afghanistan, with which we are all too familiar, which in turn has accompanied that nine-year-long military mission. It represents, in my view, a major displacement from the original, justifiable (in my judgment) reason for a military intervention in 2001, which was to roust al-Qaeda from its then-home and to oust from power its then-allies in the Taliban.

There is a disconnect between our fundamental stated purpose of protecting Americans from terrorism and the actual operational objectives of nation building and defeating the Afghan Taliban. The conflict in Afghanistan gets commonly perceived as a struggle between the [Hamid] Karzai government on the one hand and an insurgent Taliban movement allied with international terrorists. In fact, it is a civil war, which is very complicated, about how power will be shared in Afghanistan, with complicated lines of contention that run along ethnic, sectarian, urban/rural, and other lines.

A U.S. military victory over the Taliban is not a key to protecting Americans from international terrorism. This gets into some issues that were raised in the earlier panel this morning about dealing with nonstate actors. The Taliban do not constitute an international terrorist group. The Taliban represent a rural insurgency that is interested in the political and social makeup and order in Afghanistan. It is interested in the U.S. only insofar as the U.S. gets in the way of its designs for ordering Afghanistan. Al-Qaeda is barely in Afghanistan at all, as noted earlier. As David Kilcullen pointed out this morning, if [Osama] bin Laden and his leadership team were given the opportunity to return to Afghanistan, it is not at all apparent that they would see that as attractive compared to what they have in northwest Pakistan.[4] Even if it did want to return, it is doubtful that even a victorious Afghan Taliban would want it back, given what happened to the Taliban the last time it hosted the group. Back in the 1990s, you did not have a traditional patron-client relationship between a regime and a group. You had an alliance between the Taliban, which was fighting a civil war, and bin Laden's forces, which provided a lot of aid to the Taliban in fighting that civil war. There was as much giving as there was getting on the al-Qaeda end.

Al-Qaeda is not in a position to do that anymore. Even back in the 1990s when there was this mutual back-scratching and mutual help, there were plenty of signs of friction between these two groups, which, although both undeniably radical Islamists, have much different objectives, intentions, and concerns. And even if al-Qaeda or any other terrorist group attempted to establish a presence anything like bin Laden's group had prior to 2001 in Afghanistan, our rules of engagement are entirely different. We wouldn't pussyfoot around with a few cruise missile strikes like we did before; we would bomb the heck out of it. We know that, and al-Qaeda knows that, and the Taliban know that.

Even if some sort of haven were established in Afghanistan, that is simply not one of the more important things that determines the degree of threat that al-Qaeda or any other terrorist group poses to the United States. Most of the preparations for the attacks involved take place elsewhere, including especially here in the West.

---

4 Kilcullen stated that "there is certainly some al-Qaeda presence in Afghanistan now, but it's very small numbers. We often hear a discussion about how we need to prevent al-Qaeda from moving back into Afghanistan if we were to leave. I think it's highly unlikely that they would abandon a very effective safe haven in Pakistan to go to Afghanistan. I think that's a little bit of a red herring." See "Discussion of New Approaches to Nonstate Armed Actors," chapter 10 of this book. As this book was in preparation, U.S. Navy Seals killed bin Laden during a raid on his compound in Abbottabad, Pakistan, on May 2, 2011.

Although for those reasons I think some of the most basic questions in any reevaluation of policy go beyond the course of the counterinsurgency itself, one also has to bear in mind the reasons for what I think are the dim prospects for success. Stephen [Biddle] and Brian [Katulis] have both covered many of the basics extremely well. I would just note a couple things to supplement what they said.

What is the definition of "success"? I'm not sure. The numbers and force ratios required, if you open up somebody's counterinsurgency manual (like General [David H.] Petraeus's),[5] tells you that except for a few places—like, as Brian mentioned, Kandahar—if you apply that to the larger country, we simply do not have—and have absolutely no intention of committing—the resources for as long as it would take to accomplish a counterinsurgency mission.

The effort, moreover, does not have the cooperation of Pakistan, which continues to actually do business with the Afghan Taliban as an instrument of influence and a hedge against events there. Even more important, as Stephen just very forcefully described, the effort does not have an uncorrupt Afghan government with the potential for obtaining greater legitimacy than it does now.

One other thing I would add in another respect, besides the ones that Stephen mentioned, in which some of our own efforts—this time on the military side—have a counterproductive aspect. We have, through what has become an increasingly unpopular military occupation, been creating enemies probably more rapidly than we have created friends, and this in a country that had been, in the Muslim world, a welcome oasis of goodwill toward the United States. In relative terms it still is, in contrast to those poll results that Shibley Telhami presented to us in the last panel, in countries farther west in the Arab world. Much of the motivation for Taliban recruits, in addition to all the things Stephen described, has to do with resisting foreign occupation, as strongly suggested by the trajectory in estimates of Taliban strength and how that is correlated with

---

5 U.S. Army (FM 3-24) and U.S. Marine Corps (MCWP 3-33.5), *Counterinsurgency* (Washington, DC: Department of the Army and Marine Corps Combat Development Command, 2006). One of signatories on this manual was General Petraeus, who oversaw operations in Afghanistan first as head of U.S. Central Command (beginning October 2008), and subsequently as commander of the International Security Assistance Force (starting in July 2010). The other signatory was General James F. Amos, who became Commandant of the Marine Corps in October 2010. This document is more widely available as U.S. Army and Marine Corps, *The U.S. Army/Marine Corps Counterinsurgency Field Manual* (Chicago: University of Chicago Press, 2007).

our own presence there. Our own presence also encourages closer cooperation among a disparate array of extremist groups in Afghanistan and Pakistan alike. And, even more broadly, resentment over our military presence is increasing the resonance of extremist propaganda elsewhere.

I think a reevaluation of policy ought to result in a change of trajectory in three areas. One is that question of the pace of the drawdown, beginning next year, and whether it is going to be something more than just minor or cosmetic. A second area is greater openness to power-sharing and political inclusion within Afghanistan through a peace process designed to decentralize power. Here I commend and associate myself with what Brian already mentioned with regard to that subject, both its importance and the length of time it would require. I would just add to what Brian said by noting that this topic also came up in one of the panels this morning, in which a lot of cold water was thrown on the idea of negotiations. Yes, there are a lot of doubts out there about what is on the Taliban side and how serious the interest may or may not be. I would just add to this that in peace negotiations in general, you have a hard time coming up with an example in history where there wasn't a lot of dissatisfaction not just on one side but probably both sides with the particular circumstances and timing and conditions of opening talks, let alone closing a deal. As to the point that you often hear that we have to soften up the Taliban some more, bear in mind that the same logic applies to the other side. What may be the most opportune moment for us, in terms of where it is strategically most advantageous for us to talk, may not be the same moment for the other side to talk. If we forget that, we may miss an opportunity.

The third area in which policy needs to be rethought is—again, I'm just going to second what Brian said because I think he addressed it very well—a more energetic regional diplomacy to engage the stakeholders in a diplomatic effort designed to guarantee Afghan neutrality and foster regional stability.

Let me close by referring briefly to Pakistan. Something else we often hear in response to all that stuff I said about the Taliban isn't a terrorist group and so on: we're really there because of Pakistan and all those nuclear weapons, we don't want "mad mullahs" getting their hands on them, and so on. I dare say that if we started with the stability of Pakistan as a key U.S. goal in this region and did a zero-based review of how we encourage it, a counterinsurgency in Afghanistan would not be one of the measures we would take in pursuit of that objective. We have a tendency to think here in spatial terms. There is something called instability that goes over the border slowly. It's like that old Cold War imagery of red paint oozing over the globe. But if you think in more specific terms about the dynamics involved, even though there obviously is a lot of cross-border activity, that isn't really the way it works. Many of the things that we do, both on the northwest side and the southeast side of the Durand Line, because of their unpopularity, make it harder for the Pakistanis politically to cooperate with us on counterterrorism and other measures. As some Pakistani officials themselves have pointed out, to the extent that we are successful on the Afghan side in driving militants across the line, they have just got that much more of a problem on their side of the line.

The main way we ought to think about Pakistan is as a very important player in that regional diplomacy—getting the neighbors involved. The Pakistanis have made it quite clear that not only do they expect to play a very major role in whatever combination of negotiation and other processes brings about a reasonably stable end-state in Afghanistan, but also that they are quite willing and able to serve as a spoiler if they are not admitted to that kind of role. So we need to involve the Pakistanis and others in ways that reflect the considerable interests they have that parallel our own, against the backdrop of which it simply does not make sense for the U.S. by itself to bear so much of this burden.

CHAPTER NINETEEN

Pakistan–U.S. Relations

Hassan Abbas

Very clearly, the United States is still in search of a comprehensive and sustainable policy toward Pakistan. I think this was clear in some of the remarks made earlier as well. There is a disconnect, and the foundation of this disconnect is mistrust. I will come to this word "mistrust" again by the end.

What are the core U.S. security interests or core U.S. foreign policy interests in Pakistan? In my assessment, there are three. Number one, the whole issue of nuclear security. Number two, the whole notion of militancy in the tribal areas of Pakistan and the Pakistani militant groups going from the Federally Administered Tribal Areas into Afghanistan, hitting NATO and U.S. installments. The third component is an issue related to homeland security, especially since this unfortunate episode of Faisal Shahzad trying to blow up Times Square.[1] These are the three core foreign policy or national security interests of the U.S.

How does the U.S. want to deal with Pakistan, and how is it trying to deal with Pakistan? Starting with this point, I am reminded of Dennis Kux, who has written the best book on U.S.–Pakistan relations.[2] If you want to know the background, you have to read his book. But let me talk about the prevailing, current five pillars.

---

1 Shahzad attempted to set off a car bomb in Times Square in New York City on May 1, 2010 (http://topics.nytimes.com/top/reference/timestopics/people/s/faisal_shahzad/index.html).

2 Dennis Kux, *The United States and Pakistan, 1947–2000: Disenchanted Allies* (Washington, DC: Woodrow Wilson Center Press, 2001).

Number one, development aid. The Kerry-Lugar-Berman bill promises $7.5 billion in five years, $1.5 billion for development aid.[3] It is not very clearly defined what we mean by "development aid" in Pakistan, but at least we know this is not military aid, which was traditionally the case. This was in response to Pakistani critique and consistent Pakistani criticism that the U.S. always supports Pakistani military dictators, and U.S. support for Pakistan is always for military aid. In response to that, this time a different approach was taken.

The problem with that is, number one, it took quite a while. This was decided about three years ago in principal (actually, the credit goes to now-Vice President Joe Biden) but it took a couple of years really for it to go through congressional approvals and all the facilities that are needed in Pakistan. But nonetheless, development aid is the central pillar.

There are problems in that regard. One of those was referred to by Stephen Biddle when he mentioned contractor reform. Out of those $1.5 billion per year—which still has to start, except some of the amount that has gone to Pakistan for the first year[4]—people believe about $300 million will go to contractors for different bureaucratic channels. So that is a good policy that still needs a real [indiscernible] how it is implemented. But we should remember that $1.5 billion for Pakistan per year means 1 to 2 percent of its total GDP, so we are not talking about a huge amount in that sense which will make any significant change in the sociopolitical or economic fabric of the country.[5]

---

3 Commonly known by the name of its most prominent sponsors, Senators John F. Kerry and Richard G. Lugar and Congressman Howard L. Berman, the *Enhanced Partnership with Pakistan Act of 2009* provides $1.5 billion per year in aid to Pakistan for the years 2010 through 2014. *Enhanced Partnership with Pakistan Act of 2009*, Public Law 111-73, 111th Cong., 1st sess., October 15, 2009, http://www.gpo.gov/fdsys/pkg /BILLS-111s1707enr/pdf/BILLS-111s1707enr.pdf.

4 A U.S. Government Accountability Office report found that the U.S. only disbursed $179.5 million in the 2010 fiscal year. U.S. Government Accountability Office, "Department of State's Report to Congress and U.S. Oversight of Civilian Assistance to Pakistan Can Be Further Enhanced," February 27, 2011, http://www.gao.gov/new.items/d11310r.pdf.

5 According the World Bank's World Development Indicators, Pakistan's gross domestic product (GDP) in 2009 was $162 billion, in U.S. dollars (http://data.worldbank.org/data-catalog/world-development-indicators).

The second pillar of U.S. policy toward Pakistan is engagement with the Pakistan military. That is evident from what Brian [Katulis] was referring to. Between 2002 to 2008—actually before that, since [Pervez] Musharraf came into power, 2001 to 2008—$15 billion [has gone to the Pakistani military]. When I go to different areas in Pakistan, in the tribal areas, especially North-West Frontier Province (which is now called Khyber-Pakhtunkhwa), you ask people there, what was something new that was created in those eight or nine years, they cannot show you roads or hospitals or schools. We really don't know where that $15 billion went, perhaps supporting the Pakistan military in the tribal areas, enhancing its capacity.

So that relationship continues, though in a different manner. Recently, $2 billion were committed, just two or three weeks ago, in a strategic dialogue with Pakistan, $2 billion for five years. But there are serious challenges. My argument is that even if you increase that $2 billion to $20 billion, the Pakistan military has a different way of looking at its interests in the region. The Haqqani network in North Waziristan, that is an issue for the United States, for Afghans. For Pakistan, that means hedging its bets. Lashkar-e-Taiba—I fully agree that the Pakistan military, especially General Musharraf, had clamped down on so many of these terrorist groups, but not on Lashkar-e-Taiba. Even since the Mumbai attacks in 2008, where there was a very clear linkage to Lashkar-e-Taiba, some of the offices were closed, but that group remains operative, functional, active. One of the people, Mr. [Zaki ur Rehman] Lakhvi, who is considered the brain behind the Mumbai attacks (or at least one of them), is in a Pakistani prison, but the legal case is not being pursued. He apparently, according to Pakistani media reports, has his own cell phone and talks to his people.

The point I am making is that engagement with the military is good, it is vital for U.S. interests because the Pakistan military is the most central, important institution. But there is a limit to the convergence of interests. The Pakistan military has its own—from their point of view—legitimate interests. Unless we are ready to compromise, from a

U.S. perspective, on those interests, no amount of engagement or aid to the military will help.

The third pillar of U.S. policy is support for democracy. Recently, President [Asif Ali] Zardari perhaps was saved through U.S. intervention.[6] The military wanted him removed. Not the removal of the whole democratic setup, but at least his removal was in the cards. But we have to be clear that the real test will come if and when the Pakistan military will take over the country again. It is unlikely now. I hope that will not happen. But the test will also be when someone who is not very friendly toward the United States—maybe like Nawaz Sharif, maybe Imran Khan, or somebody else—will be in power. Will the U.S. still be able to say that one of our objectives in the region is to support Pakistani democracy? That will be the real test.

We have to be careful. In the case of allies and friends also, the U.S. should not push its friends too much. One incident—a tragic one—which comes to my mind is when the previous U.S. administration pushed Musharraf and Benazir Bhutto to join hands. Musharraf was a sinking ship and Benazir Bhutto was the leader of the—comparatively—most progressive political party in Pakistan. Just because of some interests in Washington, D.C., both were forced to join hands. Musharraf was going down anyway, perhaps no one could see that in Washington, D.C. Benazir Bhutto went down with him. So if that is what is meant by supporting democracy, that can be fatal.[7] So we have to be careful.

The fourth foreign policy pillar of the U.S. toward Pakistan is in fact one which is a laudable one: helping Pakistan in times of crisis. Here are two examples: the 2005 earthquake and U.S. support (not in billions, in millions) made a lot of difference, and

---

6 See Jane Perlez, "Generals in Pakistan Push for Shake-Up of Government," *New York Times*, September 28, 2010, http://www.nytimes.com/2010/09/29/world/asia/29pstan.html.

7 The "join hands" reference is metaphorical. The George W. Bush administration had attempted to broker power-sharing arrangements between Musharraf and Bhutto, a former prime minister who was well connected in Washington, throughout much of 2007. Bhutto returned from exile to Pakistan in October of that year to lead her party's challenge to Musharraf in the 2008 elections. She was assassinated on December 27, 2007, while leaving a campaign rally. Her widower, Zardari, became the party leader and succeeded Musharraf as president in 2008. Helene Cooper and Steven Lee Myers, "Salvaging U.S. Diplomacy Amid Division," *New York Times*, December 28, 2007, http://www.nytimes.com/2007/12/28 /world/asia/28policy.html; Elizabeth Bumiller, "How Bhutto Won Washington," *New York Times*, December 30, 2007, http://www.nytimes.com/2007/12/30/weekinreview /30bumiller.html.

even now that is referred to as something which changed public opinion in Pakistan toward the U.S. And recently, the 2010 devastating floods, billions of dollars of losses, a major crisis in Pakistan—the U.S. was the first country to help Pakistan, and is now providing $350 million—more than China, more than Saudi Arabia.[8] So that is the fourth pillar of this policy, which I think should stay there.

The last pillar is the most controversial one: the policy of drone attacks. The drone policy I am referring to is the unmanned aircraft which go into the Federally Administered Tribal Areas. We hear there was an attack in North Waziristan or South Waziristan or Bajaur; 10 people killed, 20 people killed, 10 terrorists killed. I believe that these drone attacks were a good tactic, but it has been converted into a strategy. So the question is whether these drone attacks are actually damaging the networks of terrorists, are creating fear among those. The answer is yes.

The second question is whether these drone attacks are popular in Pakistan. No. So can we deduce from these two that all Pakistanis probably like these terrorists, because they don't like these attacks, and these attacks are actually damaging terrorists? We cannot deduce that Pakistanis don't like these drone attacks. The reason is when there are more drone attacks, those terror networks react through Tehrik-e-Taliban Pakistan inside Pakistan. There were 95 suicide attacks in Pakistan in 2009. This year, 2010, there have been about 50 attacks or so. In 2008, [there were] 69 attacks; 2007, 66 attacks; 2005, 6 attacks.

The point I am making: just look at the increase in the number of drones, and there are more suicide attacks across Pakistan. Unprecedented things are happening, [such as] attacks on Sufi shrines in Pakistan, from Abdullah Shah Ghazi in Karachi—a very popular, well-known Sufi shrine—to the one in Peshawar of Rahman Baba, one in Lahore, one in another part of Punjab. There is a reaction from these militant groups.

8 For a broad look at the flood relief efforts, with references as well to the impact on U.S.–Pakistani relations as a result of earthquake relief efforts in 2005, see Kenneth H. Williams, ed., "The International Response to the 2010 Pakistan Flood: An Interview with Michael Young of the International Rescue Committee," *Marine Corps University Journal* 2 (Spring 2011): 81–99.

So how will we find a way that these drone attacks, which are killing terrorists—don't take me wrong, they are killing attacks—but by and large, there are also civilian casualties. So what is the net result? There is no way to quantify it, there is no empirical evidence to prove what I am saying. But it is very clear that we are creating more terrorists in the process. So in the long-term context, in my assessment, this is a counter-productive policy.

So these are the five major policy pillars. Where do we need adjustment?

Number one, I have not found any reference, I mean, I have mentioned these as the five pillars, but I think based on my reading, my research, and my interviews, both in Islamabad and in Washington, that these are in fact the five pillars. What is missing in there is a linkage to civil society actors. Unlike in Afghanistan, where it was very rightly mentioned that there are no capable, trained administrators or civil society actors, in Pakistan there are. In 2007 to 2009, they showed this by coming on the streets in support of the lawyers' movement. Hundreds of thousands of these people came on the streets, defying Musharraf and the law enforcement agencies. There are strong groups. Most recently Asma Jahangir, a lady who is a well-known human rights activist, won a very important election of the supreme court bar. The point I am making [is that] there are those civil society actors who have the potential to really make a change. I don't see the five pillars of U.S. policy supporting or strengthening them in any way.

There is a second inadequacy. I mentioned three core U.S. national security interests: loose nukes, militants in the tribal areas, and homeland security interests from the Pakistani diaspora. One way to tackle these is through police reforms. Unlike Afghan police or Iraqi police, there has been an internal demand for police reform in Pakistan. There is capacity. (I have a bias, because before my academic career, I was a police officer in Pakistan.) But my interviews tell me that there is a lot of effort. Police reforms will help the rule of law, and rule of law will help democracy. So that should be taken [into account].

There are two other adjustments I would suggest. One is de-radicalization. Yes, progressive religious leaders in Pakistan are being murdered and assassinated. But that vacuum is being filled continuously. If you want to at least hear one of those people who can really do something for de-radicalization in Pakistan, that is a well-known Pakistani writer [Muhammad Tahir-ul-Qadri], who is actually speaking here on November 8. He has given a 600-page fatwa against suicide bombing, a leading scholar.[9] There are others, like [indiscernible] as well.

Last but not least, there is the whole issue of regional context. If we continue to look at it as an Af-Pak thing and miss the fact that Pakistan formulates its policy because of India, whether we like it or not, that remains an important issue.

As [Palestinian Authority diplomat] Saeb Erakat said very rightly, there are things we are told are not possible. But then there are things that are needed. The involvement of India and Pakistan in the peace process is needed for security in Afghanistan, for peace in Pakistan. I will close with this one quote of President [Barack H.] Obama, when he said in Cairo that one way to build the foundation of this new relationship between the United States and the Middle East and the Muslim world is to build it on trust, common interest or mutual interests, and mutual respect.[10] I think that is the only way forward for a progressive, fruitful, and sustainable relationship between the U.S. and the Muslim world, including Pakistan.

---

9 Muhammad Tahir-ul-Qadri, *Fatwa on Suicide Bombings and Terrorism* (London: Minhaj-ul-Quran International, 2010; online at http://www.scribd.com/doc/29876438/Fatwa-on-Terrorism-by-Dr-Muhammad-Tahir-ul-Qadri); see also the site associated with the book and Tahir-ul-Qadri's efforts (http://www.fatwaonterrorism.com/).

10 Office of the White House Press Secretary, "Remarks by the President on a New Beginning," Cairo University, Cairo, Egypt, June 4, 2009, http://www.whitehouse.gov/the-press-office/remarks-president-cairo-university-6-04-09.

CHAPTER TWENTY

DISCUSSION OF U.S. POLICY IN AFGHANISTAN AND PAKISTAN

MODERATED BY CAROLINE WADHAMS

Question: I have a question for Stephen Biddle and Paul Pillar. It seems that a repeated theme of this conference has been that we should look at issues and conflicts in the region with a comprehensive view, taking into consideration not just one conflict or country, but the larger view. It seems to me that U.S. military policy in Afghanistan and Iraq for the past decade has been myopic, in the sense that we will attack terrorist strongholds, kill some of the terrorists; other terrorists flee from that area and move to another one. An example, if my facts are correct, [Osama] bin Laden was in Sudan before 9/11; the U.S. put pressure on Sudan, and he fled to Afghanistan. He has now fled to Pakistan. I guess my question is—and if my appraisal is wrong, please let me know—where will the terrorists go if the U.S. military is successful in getting them to leave Pakistan? In your opinion, does the U.S. government have a long-term strategy for dealing with this sort of global terrorist movement?

Question: The panel indicated that there are really bizarre things that happen when you inject $50 billion into a developing economy. It creates a bizarre set of incentives that embolden various nefarious, predatory networks. It's part of the broader COIN [counterinsurgency] strategy, that's why we do it. Is there a better way to do it, or should we do something different? If we don't inject that much money, what should we be doing instead?

Paul R. Pillar: Let me respond to the first question. I hope Steve will address more the second one. I agree very much with the premise of the question, about myopic (as you put it) counterterrorist operations. I would sort of rephrase your premise in a way that I have spoken and written about a lot, which is this is not a territorially defined problem, even though we Americans tend to think of it that way.[1]

There is no limit to answers to your specific question about where would the terrorists go. If it wasn't Sudan, it's Afghanistan. If it's not Afghanistan, it's Pakistan. If it's not Pakistan, it's Yemen. If it's not Yemen, it's someplace else. The point I tried to make earlier was that if you look at what terrorist groups—be they al-Qaeda or somebody else—do to actually prepare for attacks that would cause us the most harm—and I would put the 9/11 plot right at the top of that list—most of the preparation is not based on a chunk of real estate that is bombable or subject to a COIN campaign. Much of it is right here in the West in cities or, if it's not in the West, it's in other places, urban areas, that are not suitable military targets.[2]

Stephen D. Biddle: I guess I'll start with the $50 billion question and move to the issue of terrorists and their movements.

I don't think the issue is how much money we're spending, to be honest; I think it's how it is being used and who it is being paid to. If the choice before us is simply one of do we spend the amount of money we're spending now in the way we are or do we just shut it off, I would actually prefer shutting it off. I don't think that's the actual choice we face. I think the key requirement is that we do a better job of understand-

1 See, for example, Paul R. Pillar, "Who's Afraid of a Terrorist Haven?" *Washington Post*, September 16, 2009, http://www.washingtonpost.com/wp-dyn/content/article/2009/09/15/AR2009091502977.html; Pillar, "Counterterrorism and Stability in Afghanistan," Statement to the Committee on Armed Services, U.S. House of Representatives, October 14, 2009, http://cpass.georgetown.edu/center/publications/other/.

2 See Paul R. Pillar, "The Diffusion of Terrorism," *Mediterranean Quarterly* 21 (Winter 2010): 1-14; Pillar, "The Evolving Terrorist Threat to the U.S. Homeland," Statement to the Subcommittee on Intelligence, Information Sharing, and Terrorism Risk Assessment, Committee on Homeland Security, U.S. House of Representatives, November 19, 2009, http://cpass.georgetown.edu/center/publications/other/. For additional commentary by Pillar, see his blogspot at the *National Interest* (http://nationalinterest.org/blog/paul-pillar).

ing to whom we are paying this money and what is the subcontracting structure behind the people to whom we are paying this money, and are we paying people who are empowering and enabling a patronage network that is undermining our prospects in the war, or are we paying and enabling people who are outside that network and whose effects are potentially benign or helpful? So when I say "contracting reform," I mean "reform" advisedly, not just the end of contracting. I think we need to do the intelligence work to understand how our money is being used and to whom it is being paid.

Just a quick word with respect to the issue of terrorism. Paul and I disagree with respect to the role of geography in this problem. The central reason why I think we disagree, though I'll leave it to Paul to determine whether he agrees with me or not, is that I think it's terribly important to disaggregate terrorism into forms that are sufficiently virulent that they require major expenditure of effort on our part to deal with and forms that are much less virulent and that at the end of the day, we are going to have to learn to live with. One of the central distinguishers between the former and the latter is the prospective use of weapons of mass destruction. The reason why I worry about Pakistan in ways that I do not frankly worry about Yemen, Somalia, Djibouti, and all the rest is because Pakistan has a nuclear arsenal, the others do not. In the event that the Pakistani state were to collapse as a result of failure in its internal war, I could imagine scenarios in which a breakup of the Pakistani military and intelligence service could result in the transfer of usable weapons to a terrorist organization that might very well use them against us.

In that context, I am much less worried about the movement of terrorists across borders around the world, and I'm much more worried about the specific problem of the stability of Pakistan. The reason I care about Afghanistan is not primarily because it could potentially be a base for Osama bin Laden in the way that it was in 2001. It is primarily because states are ordinarily concerned with the stability of their neighbors when it comes to their own internal stability. We worry, heaven knows, tremendously about the role of Pakistani safe havens in undermining the stability of the government in Kabul. I actually think the more severe problem is in the long run the opposite direction.

The whole U.S. involvement in the Balkans in the 1980s and 1990s was driven to a large degree by concern with the effect of stability in the Balkans on stability in trading partners and NATO allies of ours in Europe. The reason that the issue of Mexico is getting the attention in the American public debate that it now does is because of a concern that instability can in fact have negative effects across borders.

Reasonable people can disagree as to whether the scale of investment we are now making in Afghanistan is commensurate with the scale of that threat. I have argued elsewhere that on the analytic merits, it is a rather close call because the nature of our security interests are primarily indirect in this sense, with respect to Afghanistan, and the costs of waging the war obviously are high. But I think it is the case that if you wanted to make an argument for the necessity of being involved in Afghanistan, it would lie principally in Afghanistan's effects on Pakistan, and this is not a bizarre or idiosyncratic argument that does not in fact affect international politics normally around the globe, which in fact I think it does.[3]

Question: My question is in response to Brian's comment that there are varying reports in the U.S. media in regard to progress of the Afghan strategy. With that said, what are the critical metrics that can accurately measure whether we are successful or failing in Afghanistan?

Question: During the summer, there was a lot of talk about trying to root out corruption. It became more highlighted in the press, I think. Toward the end of the summer, maybe September, there were several articles saying that we were going to try to shift focus away from trying to push them so much, because there was resistance from [Afghan President Hamid] Karzai, and instead try to work through the top of the

---

3 For additional commentary by Biddle on many of the points that he covered, see his page at the Council on Foreign Relations (http://www.cfr.org/experts/afghanistan-iraq-terrorism/stephen-biddle/b2603).

government to have them root out the corruption quietly, going through the ranks themselves and trusting them to do that.

A lot of the panelists talked about corruption, trying to go from the bottom up. Do you see any possibility that that quiet, top-down approach will work or help, or will it be counterproductive?

Question: What do you think the prospects are for our getting the Pakistanis to shut down the use of FATA [Federally Administered Tribal Areas] and other border areas as a safe haven for the militants? If we fail, what are our prospects for success in Afghanistan?

Question: Mine is a two-pronged question. One is relating to the infrastructure buildup. Would you agree that we have overly relied on contractors, both in terms of local strongmen who we give the money to spread out and build the sewer system, as opposed to a plain old-fashioned, New Deal-type WPA [Works Progress Administration] where the goal was to spread out the money to the maximum degree? A quick thumb-nail calculation indicates that we could pay every Afghan male $3,000 a year for the mere sum of $30 billion a year. Would that be more effective?

The add-on to this question is, in something like northwest Pakistan, to shut down the madrassas—I'm just beginning to throw out a wild idea here—but if the kids go there to get food, why don't we just take a hundred old planes out of the desert, jetliners, load them up with MREs [meal, ready to eat], and fly over there every day as a regular school lunch run, and meanwhile include some MP3 players that have the Qur'an on there and some benign interpretations. That way they could learn the Qur'an, they could get fed, and they wouldn't be in madrassas.

Caroline Wadhams: Thank you. We'll start with Brian for the first question on metrics.

Brian Katulis: And maybe Steve can jump in here. I think part of one thing that Paul said, in terms of our goal and end-state and the lack of clarity of it—and this is something that has concerned me for a while—which feeds into the metrics. The president has been quite right to articulate a broader goal of disrupt, dismantle, and defeat al-Qaeda in Afghanistan and Pakistan. The question of what that actually means in terms of what we need to build, to leave behind, to achieve that is still unanswered both within government and within the larger analytical community here. I don't know if anyone disagrees with that.

But that end-state question—which we have raised in reports,[4] and others have—hampers the ability to measure them if you don't know what you're trying to build. We have a decent metric in terms of how many Afghan national security forces we want to have by 2011, 2012, and 2013. I think there is some way to measure the progress in terms of their capacity, numbers, and ability and willingness to stay in the fight. Those critical metrics in building are much stronger on the security side.

On the governance side, I think this is very much a work in progress. We need greater clarity. But when you get down to it, if you are looking at it from a COIN framework, it is not captures and kills, it is how secure does the population feel. Maybe Stephen can add to this. There are various metrics that look at how long do markets stay open and a range of issues, and you can really get deep into it largely based on how safe the population feels.

But circling back, in absence of a broader, clearly defined end-state to help us achieve that goal of disrupt, dismantle, and defeat al-Qaeda in both countries, we still will be wallowing in this sense of we're not sure if we're doing better or worse. There will be various narratives that will try to frame our debate here, much in the way that we saw in Iraq. Security has improved in Iraq, but a lot of the things in terms of basic services and the capacity of the government to deliver, or the political grievances that divide societies like in Iraq, endure even after the military success of the surge.

---

4 See Caroline Wadhams, Colin Cookman, Brian Katulis, and Lawrence Korb, "Realignment: Managing a Stable Transition to Afghan Responsibility: Recommendations for the United States and Its Allies" (Center for American Progress, November 2010; online at http://www.americanprogress.org/issues /2010/11/pdf/afghanistanleadership.pdf). For additional commentary by Katulis, see his page at the Center for American Progress (http://www.americanprogress.org/experts/KatulisBrian.html).

So this is the place where we need more critical thinking, and it is particularly on the government capacity side.

Biddle: Just a very quick point on metrics and end-states, and then a quick point on contractors. Brian is absolutely right—the end-state debate is underdeveloped. I do think there are obtainable, acceptable end-states one can articulate for Afghanistan. I commend to your attention a piece that (with two coauthors) I wrote in *Foreign Affairs* two issues ago that seeks to define what is the intersection between the acceptable and the achievable with respect to ultimate political conditions in Afghanistan.[5] We argue that there are several, differentiated largely by the scale of decentralization of governance in the country, any of which involve walking back to an important degree from the extremely ambitious end-state goals that the [George W.] Bush administration adopted, which were ambitious to the point of unfeasibility. But there are ways of walking back that get us into the domain of the feasible but leave us within the domain of the acceptable. We can talk about specific metrics along the way to get there.

Let me just suggest very briefly, though, that if you believe that governance reform is critical in order to get to any of these end-states, which I think it is, the key is measuring how well or badly we are doing on that. That requires intelligence work to do things like uncover the size of the illicit economy, determine what the current payment required to get a district police chief job in Kandahar is this year compared to last year. I think there are a variety of things that can tell you quite a bit about how you're doing and are not in principal unknowable, but which will require a substantial redirection of our intelligence system and its current priorities.

Let me briefly close with a word on contractors. Absolutely, we are overreliant on contractors. One of the central dimensions of military activity required to get governance reform is one of the primary ways in which we are dependent on contractors right now: to deliver the logistical resources required to keep our military functioning and to pro-

---

5 Stephen Biddle, Fotini Christia, and J. Alexander Thier, "Defining Success in Afghanistan," *Foreign Affairs*, July–August 2010.

vide the security for the convoys that move those resources around the country. At the moment, this is done, overwhelmingly, with local contracting. The local contractors who do this, especially providing the security, create in effect private armies for the use of the networks we are dealing with to act as the muscle to enforce their edicts with the local population. This is tremendously undermining of our success in the undertaking. If we are going to deal with it, it is probably going to require that we are going to have to take military assets out of orthodox population security and put them into logistical activity, especially securing that logistical activity.

One of the reasons why governance reform is in fact a military mission with important costs and trade-offs against the conduct of security operations is because if we continue to insist on the use of contractors to provide the support for that security activity, we will make governance improvement, in all likelihood, impossible. There is a trade-off that requires some choices, and I think we are going to have to make those choices in favor of prioritizing governance activity with respect to the use of our military resources in ways that we have not in the past.

Wadhams: Paul, do you think you could pick up on the question about approaching Karzai more quietly on the corruption issues?

Pillar: I was going to use my last minute just to compliment one of the other questioners on his creativity about things like air drops and MREs and MP3 players, a $3,000 stipend. Whether those are good ideas or not, I think it is a useful way of making the point and underscoring the point that all too little attention has been given to this war in cost-benefit terms, exactly what the costs are and what we are buying with that. Perhaps some of these ideas would be a better way.

Hassan Abbas: I think it is unfortunately, tragically, quite unlikely that Pakistan will be able to tackle the tribal areas in the next five to seven years. It is partly fear, it is partly incompetence, it is partly all those previous peace "deals" which allowed those militants to expand their influence. U.S. policy at that time was too focused on Iraq. We have no time to get into that.

But having said that, I would argue that failure in the Pakistani tribal areas, or the long time that it will take if all the right decisions are taken today—it will still take five to ten years to resolve that—that does not mean the U.S. cannot succeed in Afghanistan. All the wrongs that are taking place in Afghanistan cannot be blamed on Pakistan. One example: I seriously doubt—and this is something unconventional, against the conventional belief, but just food for thought—I very much doubt that Mullah Omar, whether he is in tribal areas in Pakistan or in Quetta or in Islamabad, that he is the one who is running insurgency in Afghanistan. No. Insurgency and militancy in Afghanistan is happening because there is a new second generation of leadership. Haqqani, yes, to some extent.

The point is, there are still ways, despite that lack of possibility of improving things in FATA, for success in Afghanistan. There are other metrics. There are other reasons that can allow that to happen.

CONTRIBUTORS

Contributors

Hassan Abbas is the Quaid-i-Azam Professor at Columbia University's South Asia Institute (http://www.sipa.columbia.edu/academics/directory/ha2278-fac.html) and a senior advisor at the Belfer Center for Science and International Affairs at Harvard University's Kennedy School of Government (http://belfercenter.ksg.harvard.edu/experts/850/hassan_abbas.html). He is Bernard Schwartz Fellow at the Asia Society and is a visiting fellow at the Islamic Legal Studies Program at Harvard Law School and a visiting scholar at the Harvard Law School's Program on Negotiation. His books include *Pakistan's Drift into Extremism: Allah, the Army and America's War on Terror* (2005) and *Pakistan's Troubled Frontier* (2009). He also runs *WATANDOST* (http://watandost.blogspot.com/), a blog on Pakistan and its neighbors' affairs. Abbas is a former Pakistani government official who served in the administrations of Prime Minister Benazir Bhutto (1995–96) and President Pervez Musharraf (1999–2000).

Geneive Abdo is director of the Iran program at the Century Foundation (http://tcf.org/about/fellows/geneive-abdo-fellow) and creator and editor of insideIRAN (http://www.insideiran.org/). Before joining the Century Foundation, she served as the liaison for the United Nation's Alliance of Civilizations. In her 20-year journalism career, Abdo covered the Middle East and the Islamic world as a correspondent in Iran for the *Guardian* and the *Economist*. She was the first American journalist to be based in Tehran in the aftermath of the 1979 Islamic Revolution and earlier reported from Egypt, Algeria, Syria, Lebanon, Iran, the Persian Gulf, Central Asia, Afghanistan, and Georgia. Abdo was a Nieman fellow at Harvard University (2001–2), the same year that she received a John Simon Guggenheim Fellowship. She is author of *Mecca and Main Street: Muslim Life in America After 9/11* (2006) and *No God but God: Egypt and the Triumph of Islam* (2000), and coauthor (with Jonathan Lyons) of *Answering Only to God: Faith and Freedom in Twenty-First Century Iran* (2003).

Stephen D. Biddle is the Roger Hertog Senior Fellow for defense policy at the Council on Foreign Relations (http://www.cfr.org/experts/afghanistan-iraq-terrorism/stephen-biddle/b2603). He has previously held positions at the U.S. Army War College's Strategic Studies Institute, the University of North Carolina at Chapel Hill, the Institute for Defense Analyses, Harvard University's Belfer Center for Science and International Affairs, and Harvard's Kennedy School of Government. In 2005, his book *Military Power: Explaining Victory and Defeat in Modern Battle* (2004) won the Council on Foreign Relations's Arthur Ross Award Silver Medal. Biddle is a member of the Defense Policy Board and has presented testimony before congressional committees on the wars in Iraq and Afghanistan, force planning, conventional net assessment, and European arms control. He has also served on military strategic assessment teams for Generals Stanley A. McChrystal and David H. Patraeus. He has been awarded Barchi, Rist, and Impact Prizes from the Military Operations Research Society, the U.S. Army Superior Civilian Service Medal, and the U.S. Army Commander's Award for Public Service in Baghdad.

Barbara K. Bodine is a lecturer in public policy and the director of the Scholars in the Nation's Service Initiative at the Woodrow Wilson School of Public and International Affairs at Princeton University (http://wws.princeton.edu/people/display_person.xml?netid=bbodine&all=yes). In her over 30 years in the U.S. Foreign Service, she served as ambassador to Yemen (1997–2001), in Baghdad as deputy principal officer during the Iran–Iraq War, in Kuwait as deputy chief of mission, and again in Iraq in 2003 as the senior State Department official and the first Coalition coordinator for reconstruction. Since leaving the government, Bodine has been senior research fellow and director of the Governance Initiative in the Middle East at Harvard University's Kennedy School of Government, a fellow at the Kennedy School's Center for Public Leadership and Institute of Politics, and the Robert Wilhelm Fellow at MIT's Center for International Studies. She is also a past president of the Mine Action Group, America, a global NGO that provides technical expertise for the removal of remnants of conflict worldwide.

Wendy J. Chamberlin has been president of the Middle East Institute since 2007 (http://www.mei.edu/Scholars/WendyChamberlin.aspx). A 29-year veteran of the U.S. Foreign Service, she was U.S. ambassador to Pakistan (2001–2) and Laos (1996–99). She also had postings in Morocco, Zaire (now the Congo), and Malaysia and served as director of global affairs and counterterrorism at the National Security Council (1991–93), deputy in the Bureau of International Counter-Narcotics and Law Programs (1999–2001), and as assistant administrator in the Asia and Near East Bureau for USAID (2002–4). Prior to joining the Middle East Institute, Chamberlin served in Geneva as deputy high commissioner for the United Nations high commissioner for refugees (2004–6).

Edward P. Djerejian is the founding director of the James A. Baker III Institute for Public Policy at Rice University in Houston (http://bakerinstitute.org/personnel/fellows-scholars/edjerejian). His career in public service began in 1962, spanned the administrations of eight U.S. presidents, and included service as U.S. ambassador to Syria (1989–91) and Israel (1993–94). Between these postings, he was assistant secretary of state for Near Eastern Affairs (1991–93). In 2006, Djerejian was a senior advisor to the Iraq Study Group, which Baker cochaired. Djerejian is author of *Danger and Opportunity: An American Ambassador's Journey through the Middle East* (2008) and is managing partner of Djerejian Global Consultancies (http://www.globalconsultancies.com/).

Roger Hardy worked for the BBC World Service for more than 20 years as a Middle East and Islamic affairs analyst. He wrote and presented a series of radio programs about the Arab–Israeli conflict, Saudi Arabia, Turkey, and the role of Islam in such diverse settings as Southeast Asia, the Middle East, and Europe. He turned his experiences into a book, *The Muslim Revolt: A Journey through Political Islam* (2010). At the time of the conference, he was a public policy scholar at the Woodrow Wilson International Center for Scholars in Washington. At the time of publication, he is a visiting fellow at the London School of Economics. He is a regular contributor to many publications, including the *Economist, International Affairs*, and the *New Statesman*.

Joost R. Hiltermann is the deputy program director of the Middle East and North Africa for the International Crisis Group (ICG) (http://www.crisisgroup.org/en/about/staff/field/mena/joost-hiltermann.aspx). Since 2002, he has managed a team of analysts based in the Middle East and North Africa to conduct research and write policy-focused reports on factors that increase the risk of and drive armed conflict. He has written extensively on Iraq for ICG, *Foreign Policy*, the *New York Review of Books*, and other publications. Prior to joining ICG, he was executive director of the Arms Division of Human Rights Watch. His most recent book is *A Poisonous Affair: America, Iraq, and the Gassing of Halabja* (2007).

Brian Katulis is a senior fellow at the Center for American Progress, where his work focuses on U.S. national security policy in the Middle East and South Asia (http://www.americanprogress.org/experts/KatulisBrian.html). He has served as a consultant to numerous U.S. government agencies, private corporations, and NGOs on projects in more than two dozen countries, including Iraq, Pakistan, Afghanistan, Yemen, Egypt, and Colombia. From 1995 to 1998, he lived and worked in the West Bank and Gaza Strip and Egypt for the National Democratic Institute for International Affairs. In 1994–95, he was a Fulbright scholar in Amman, Jordan, where he conducted research on the peace treaty between Israel and Jordan. He is coauthor (with Nancy E. Soderberg) of *The Prosperity Agenda: What the World Wants from America—and What We Need in Return* (2008). He blogs on the AfPak Channel of the *Foreign Affairs* site (http://afpak.foreignpolicy.com/blog/5087) and in The Arena at *Politico* (http://www.politico.com/arena/bio/brian_katulis.html).

David Kilcullen is a nonresident senior fellow at the Center for a New American Security (http://www.cnas.org/node/539) and president and CEO of Caerus Associates (http://caerusassociates.com/). He was previously special advisor for counterinsurgency to Secretary of State Condoleezza Rice and a senior counterinsurgency advisor to General David H. Petraeus when he commanded Multi National Force–Iraq. In 2005–6, Kilcullen was chief counterterrorism strategist at the U.S. Department of State and helped design and implement the Regional Strategic Initiative, the policy that drives U.S. counterterrorism diplomacy worldwide. From 2004 to 2005, he was seconded to the Pentagon, where he wrote the counterterrorism strategy for the 2006 U.S. Quadrennial Defense Review. A former Australian infantry officer with 22 years of service, Kilcullen holds several honors and decorations, including the U.S. Army Superior Civilian Service Medal, the first such award given to a foreign national serving in combat alongside U.S. forces. He has published two recent books, *The Accidental Guerrilla: Fighting Small Wars in the Midst of a Big One* (2009) and *Counterinsurgency* (2010).

David Makovsky is the Ziegler Distinguished Fellow and director of the Washington Institute For Near East Policy's project on the Middle East peace process (http://www.washingtoninstitute.org/templateC10.php?CID=6). He is also an adjunct lecturer in Middle East Studies at Johns Hopkins University's School of Advanced International Studies. He is a member of the Council on Foreign Relations and the London-based International Institute for Strategic Studies. Makovsky is author of a variety of publications on the Arab–Israeli conflict, including his latest book (with Dennis Ross), *Myths, Illusions, and Peace: Finding a New Direction for America in the Middle East* (2009). Before joining the Washington Institute, he covered the peace process from 1989 to 2000 as a journalist. He is the former executive editor of the *Jerusalem Post*, was diplomatic correspondent for Israel's leading daily, *Haaretz*, and is a former contributing editor to *U.S. News and World Report*.

Robert Malley is the Middle East and North Africa program director for the International Crisis Group (ICG) (http://www.crisisgroup.org/en/about/staff/field/mena/robert-malley.aspx). He directs analysts based in Amman, Cairo, Beirut, Tel Aviv, and Baghdad. Together they report on the political, social, and economic factors affecting the risk of conflict and make policy recommendations to address these threats. Malley covers events from Iran to Morocco, with a heavy focus on the Arab–Israeli conflict, Iraq, and Islamist movements throughout the region, as well as developments in the United States that affect policy toward the Middle East. Prior to his work at ICG, Malley was special assistant to President William J. Clinton for Arab–Israeli affairs (1998–2001); executive assistant to National Security Advisor Samuel R. Berger (1996–98); and director for democracy, human rights, and humanitarian affairs at the National Security Council (1994–96).

Suzanne Maloney is a senior fellow at the Saban Center for Middle East Policy at the Brookings Institution, where her research focuses on energy, economic reform, and U.S. policy toward the Middle East (http://www.brookings.edu/experts/maloneys.aspx). She published *Iran's Long Reach: Iran as a Pivotal State in the Muslim World* in 2008 and is working on a book project on Iran's political economy since the Islamic Revolution. Prior to joining Brookings, Maloney was a member of the State Department's policy planning staff, covering Iran, Iraq, the Persian Gulf states, and broader Middle East issues. Her career includes positions at ExxonMobil Corporation, where she worked on regional business development, political risk analysis, and corporate outreach and communications. Maloney also directed the 2004 Council on Foreign Relations Task Force on U.S. Policy toward Iran, chaired by Zbigniew Brzezinski and Robert M. Gates.

Peter R. Neumann is a senior lecturer in War Studies at King's College London (http://www.kcl.ac.uk/sspp/departments/warstudies/people/lecturers/neumann.aspx). He is codirector of the master's degree program in terrorism, security, and society and the director of the International Centre for the Study of Radicalization and Political Violence (http://icsr.info/page/Peter-Neumann---Director). His books include *Old and New Terrorism: Late Modernity, Globalization, and the Transformation of Political Violence* (2009); *The Strategy of Terrorism: How it Works, and Why it Fails* (2008, coauthored with M. L. R. Smith); and *Britain's Long War: British Strategy in the Northern Ireland Conflict, 1969–98* (2003). Neumann is a member of the Club de Madrid's expert advisory council as well as of the editorial boards of *Studies in Conflict and Terrorism and Democracy and Security*. He is an affiliate of the European Commission's European Network of Experts on Radicalization and serves as a member of the German Federal Criminal Office's European Expert Network on Terrorism Issues.

Paul R. Pillar is a visiting professor and director of graduate studies of the Security Studies Program in the Edmund A. Walsh School of Foreign Service at Georgetown University (http://explore.georgetown.edu/people/prp8/?Action=View&PageTemplateID=93). He retired in 2005 from a 28-year career in the U.S. intelligence community, in which his last position was national intelligence officer for the Near East and South Asia. Earlier, he served in a variety of analytical and managerial positions, including as chief of analytic units at the CIA covering portions of the Near East, the Persian Gulf, and South Asia. Pillar also served on the National Intelligence Council as one of the original members of its Analytic Group. He has been executive assistant to the CIA's deputy director for intelligence and executive assistant to Director of Central Intelligence William H. Webster. He has also headed the Assessments and Information Group of the DCI Counterterrorist Center and from 1997 to 1999 was deputy chief of the center. He was a Federal Executive Fellow at the Brookings Institution in

1999–2000. Pillar is a retired officer in the U.S. Army Reserve and served on active duty in 1971–73, including a tour of duty in Vietnam. His books include *Terrorism and U.S. Foreign Policy* (2001) and *Negotiating Peace: War Termination as a Bargaining Process* (1983). He blogs at the *National Interest* (http://nationalinterest.org/blog/paul-pillar).

Itamar Rabinovich is a former Israeli ambassador to the United States (1993–96) and chief negotiator with Syria (1992–95). He is Distinguished Global Professor of Hebrew and Judaic Studies at New York University (http://as.nyu.edu/object/aboutas.global-professor.ItamarRabinovich), a professor of Middle East history at Tel Aviv University (http://www.itamarrabinovich.tau.ac.il/), and Charles Bronfman Distinguished Non-resident Senior Fellow at the Brookings Institution's Saban Center (http://www.brook-ings.edu/experts/rabinovichi.aspx). He served as president of Tel Aviv University from 1999 to 2007. Rabinovich is also a senior research fellow at that university's Moshe Dayan Center for Middle Eastern and African Studies and coeditor of the center's new review journal, *Bustan* (http://www.brill.nl/bustan-middle-east-book-review). He is the author of numerous books on the modern history and politics of the Middle East, the most recent of which is *The View from Damascus: State, Political Community and Foreign Relations in Twentieth-Century Syria* (2008).

Mitchell B. Reiss is president of Washington College in Chestertown, Maryland (http://president.washcoll.edu/mitchellreiss/). Previously, he was the diplomat-in-residence at the College of William and Mary, where he held a number of leadership positions. From 2003 to 2007, Reiss served as President George W. Bush's special envoy for the Northern Ireland peace process with the rank of ambassador. He was also director of the Office of Policy Planning at the U.S. Department of State (2003–5). Earlier service included postings as special assistant to the national security advisor at the

White House and consultant to the U.S. Arms Control and Disarmament Agency, the Congressional Research Service, and Los Alamos National Laboratory. Reiss has published widely on issues of international trade, security, and arms control. His most recent book is *Negotiating with Evil: When to Talk to Terrorists* (2010).

Ömer Taşpınar is director of the Turkey Project at the Brookings Institution as well as a nonresident senior fellow of foreign policy (http://www.brookings.edu/experts/taspinaro.aspx). He is a professor at the National War College and an adjunct professor at Johns Hopkins University's School of Advanced International Studies. Taşpınar is an expert on Turkey, the European Union, Muslims in Europe, political Islam, the Middle East, and Kurdish nationalism. He has held consulting positions at the Robert F. Kennedy Center for Human Rights and at the Strategic Planning Department of TOFAS-FIAT in Istanbul. Taşpınar is author of *Kurdish Nationalism and Political Islam in Turkey: Kemalist Identity in Transition* (2005) and *Fighting Radicalism with Human Development: Education and Growth in the Islamic World* (2004), and coauthor (with Philip H. Gordon) of *Winning Turkey: How America, Europe, and Turkey Can Revive a Fading Partnership* (2008).

Shibley Telhami holds the Anwar Sadat Chair for Peace and Development at the University of Maryland, College Park (http://sadat.umd.edu/people/shibley_telhami.htm) and is a nonresident senior fellow at the Saban Center at the Brookings Institution (http://www.brookings.edu/experts/telhamis.aspx). He has served as advisor to the U.S. Mission to the United Nations, as advisor to former Congressman Lee Hamilton, as a member of the U.S. delegation to the Trilateral U.S.–Israeli–Palestinian Anti-Incitement Committee, and as an advisor to the U.S. Department of State. He also served on the Iraq Study Group as a member of the Strategic Environment Working Group.

Telhami is an expert on U.S. policy in the Middle East, particularly on the role of the news media in shaping political identity and public opinion in the region, and is completing a book titled *Reflections of Hearts and Minds: Media, Opinion, and Identity in the Arab World*. Other works by him include *The Stakes: America and the Middle East: The Consequences of Power and the Choice for Peace* (2002), *Power and Leadership in International Bargaining: The Path to the Camp David Accords* (1990), and several coedited books. Telhami is a member of the Council on Foreign Relations and serves on the board of the Education for Employment Foundation.

Alex Vatanka, a scholar with the Middle East Institute (http://www.mei.edu/Scholars/AlexVatanka.aspx), is editor of Jane's Islamic Affairs Analyst (http://jiaa.janes.com/public/jiaa/index.shtml). From 2001 to 2009, he was a senior analyst at Jane's, where he covered the Middle East. He also lectures as a senior fellow in Middle East Studies at the U.S. Air Force Special Operations School. His current area of focus is Iranian domestic, security, and foreign policies. He has lectured widely for both governmental and commercial audiences, including the U.S. Department State, various U.S. military branches, U.S. congressional staff, and Middle East energy firms.

Caroline Wadhams is a senior fellow at the Center for American Progress (http://www.americanprogress.org/experts/WadhamsCaroline.html). She focuses on Afghanistan, Pakistan, terrorism issues, and U.S. national security. Wadhams served as a U.S. election observer in Afghanistan's parliamentary elections in September 2010 and Pakistan's parliamentary elections in February 2008. Prior to American Progress, she was as a legislative assistant on foreign policy issues for former Senator Russ Feingold. She also worked at the Council on Foreign Relations in Washington as the assistant director for the Meetings Program and in New York as a research associate on national security issues. Her overseas experience includes work with the International Rescue Committee in Sierra Leone and two years in Ecuador and Chile. Wadhams is a 2005 Manfred Wörner Fellow with the German Marshall Fund and a term member at the Council on Foreign Relations. She has been a guest analyst with numerous media outlets, including CNN, BBC, C-SPAN, Voice of America, Al Jazeera, FOX, Reuters, and NPR.

Kenneth H. Williams is the founding senior editor for Marine Corps University Press and *Marine Corps University Journal* (http://www.tecom.usmc.mil/mcu/mcupress/) and also serves as senior editor for the U.S. Marine Corps History Division (http://www.history.usmc.mil/). A scholarly editor for more than two decades, his previous experience includes research/editorial positions at Rice University and the University of Kentucky. He has coedited six books and published numerous journal articles.

INDEX

A

Gaza: Hamas in, 3, 5, 71-75, 97, 114, 118, 125, 138; fighting in, 97; governance in, 42; humanitarian issues in, 42-43, 77; Israel fighting in (2008), 2, 74, 130, 140; U.S. and, 42-43, 77

Germany: and Afghanistan, 85; and Middle East peace process, 49; and de-radicalization programs, 85

Ghazi, Abdullah Shah, 177

Golan Heights, 124, 137

Great Britain: empire decline, 34; and IRA, 4, 59-63; and Middle East peace process, 49, 72

Greece: and Israel, 125

Green Movement (Iran), 118

Grupos Antiterroristas de Liberación (GAL), 61

Gulf Cooperation Council (GCC), 116

Gulf War (1990–91), 34

H

Haass, Richard N.: on Middle East peace process, 43-44

Hamas: and Fatah, 9-10, 41-42, 72, 74-75; in Gaza, 3, 5, 42, 71-75, 96-97, 118, 123-25, 138; governance of, 42, 93; and Iran, ix, 6-

7, 36, 41, 109, 114, 118, 123-25, 132, 138; and Israel, 42, 59; leadership of, 60; K. Meshaal and, 36, 109; and Middle East peace process, 36, 42, 74-76, 96-97; and Muslim Brotherhood; and Quartet, 42, 72, 93; and Syria, 36; and Turkey, 109, 125; and U.S., 71, 77

Haqqani Network, 149, 175

Hardy, Roger, 87, 89, 93, 98

Hariri, Rafiq, 48

Hariri, Saad, 125

Harvard University, 34

Helmand Province, Afghanistan: counterinsurgency in, 148; governance in, 158; Taliban in, 89

Herat Province, Afghanistan, 89, 149

Hezbollah: and Iran, ix, 6-7, 36, 41, 91, 109, 114, 123-25, 132, 137-38; and Israel, 37, 140; and Lebanon, 5, 36, 72-73, 90-91, 123-25, 138; and Middle East peace process, 36; Nasrallah and, 128, 140; and Palestinians, 75; popularity of, 90-91; and Syria, 36, 41, 91, 125, 137; and UN, 90; and U.S., 71, 77-78, 90-91

Hiltermann, Joost R.: on U.S. in Iraq, 3, 21-25, 45-46; on Iraq and Turkey, 50-51

Iran–Contra affair, 92

Iraq: aid in, 99; al-Qaeda in, 66; al-Anbar
Awakening in, 59, 62, 66, 68, 91-92;
CPA in, 66; de-radicalization program
in, 6, 84; governance in, 186-87; and
Iran, 3, 6, 23-25, 113-14, 123, 132-33;
and Kurds, 22-23, 46, 50; invades
Kuwait (1990), 123; oil in, 23; police
training in, 178; Saddam Hussein
and, ix, 7, 107, 113, 123; Sadrists in, 73;
Sunni tribes in, 4, 59, 62, 66, 68, 84,
91-92, 100; "surge" in, 3, 22-23, 68, 92,
187; and Turkey, 50-51, 107-8, 110,
140; UN sanctions in, 31; and U.S., 1-
3, 5, 21-25, 45-46, 59, 61-62, 66, 68,
91-92, 96, 99-100, 107-8, 123, 130-31,
152-53, 181, 186-87, 189; WMD
suspected in, 61; and Yemen, 140. *See
also* Iraq War (2003-)

Iraqiya (political party), 109

Iraq War (2003-): 2003 invasion, 3, 21;
al-Anbar Awakening, 59, 62, 66, 68,
91-92; Arab public opinion of, 130-31;
G.W. Bush and, 21-23, 27; Coalition
Provisional Authority and, 66;
de-Baathification, 22; Obama and, 1-
2; strategic framework agreement, 23;
"surge" (2008), 3, 22-23, 68, 92, 187;
transition to peace, 1-3, 5, 23-25, 45-
46, 96, 99-100, 123, 152-53, 186-87;
and weapons of mass destruction, 61

Irbil, Iraq: Turkey and, 50, 108

IRGC. *See* Islamic Revolutionary
Guard Corps

Irish Republican Army (IRA): and Great
Britain, 4, 59-63, 94; Sinn Féin, 60

ISI. *See* Inter-Services Intelligence

Islamabad, Pakistan, 152, 178

Islamic Revolutionary Guard Corps
(Iran), 4, 30, 138-39

Israel: Arab views of, ix, 110, 127-35,
140-41; Ben-Gurion and, 121-22;
Camp David Accords (1978), 133-34;
demographics of, 37; Egypt and, 10,
122, 124; and Ethiopia, 122; fighting
in Gaza (2008), 2, 74, 111, 130, 140;
and Gaza, 42, 111, 140-41; and
Greece, 125; and Hamas, 42, 59, 73;
and Hezbollah, 37, 140; and Iran, 7,
47, 121-25, 128, 138-39; and Jordan,
122; and Lebanon, 4, 48, 73-75, 111,
130, 140; and *Mavi Marmara*, 111,

140-41; and Middle East peace process, ix, 2-4, 15-19, 34, 36-37, 40-45, 49-50, 52, 121-25, 127-35, 137-38; and Middle East region, x, 6-8, 10, 37, 121-25, 127-35; and Palestinians, ix, 2-4, 15-19, 34, 36-37, 40-45, 49-50, 73-75, 124, 137; public opinion in, 137; and Saudi Arabia, 124; and Syria, 7, 40, 48-49, 111, 124, 132, 137; and Turkey, 7, 109-11, 121-25, 138; and U.S., 2, 15-19, 36-37, 40-45, 109, 122, 137-38, 140-42; West Bank settlements in, 3; Yom Kippur War (1973), 37

Istanbul, Turkey, 117, 189

J

Jahangir, Asma, 178

Japan: and Iran, 28-29

Jasmine Revolution (2011). *See* Arab Spring (2011)

Jerusalem: as Middle East peace issue, 19, 124; perspective from, 121

Jordan: Iraqi sheikhs in, 91; and Iran, 132; and Israel, 122; public opinion in, 127-35, 140; and U.S., 127, 141

K

Kabul, Afghanistan, 67, 184

Kadima Party (Israel), 18

Kandahar Province, Afghanistan: counter-insurgency in, 148, 168; governance in, 150, 158, 187; malign actors in, 159-60, 162

Karachi, Pakistan: shrine attacked in, 177

Karzai, Ahmed Wali, 162

Karzai, Hamid: and corruption, 162, 184-85, 188; and NATO summit (2010), 148; and reforms, 150; and Taliban, 166; and U.S., 162; as weak leader, 67

Kashmir: India–Pakistan conflict over, 36, 46

Katulis, Brian: on U.S. in Afghanistan and Pakistan, 8, 147-55, 186-87; mentioned, 168-69, 187

Kenya, 98

Kerry, John F.: and Pakistan aid bill, 152, 174

Khamenei, Sayyed Ali Hoseyni: leadership of, 39, 115, 119; U.S. and, 28, 142

Khan, Imran, 176

Khatami, Sayyed Mohammad: as Iranian

Middle East peace process, 2-3, 15-19, 34, 36, 42-45, 49-50; mentioned, 76

Malley, Robert: on Hamas, 71-78; on Hezbollah, 71-78, 90-91; on Middle East peace process, 16, 71-78, 96-97; on U.S. and nonstate actors, 5, 71-78, 98

Maloney, Suzanne: on Iran, 3-4, 27-31, 39-41, 47-48, 51-52

Manningham-Buller, Eliza, 58

March 14 Alliance: and Hezbollah, 77; in Lebanon, 72, 75, 77; U.S. and, 75, 77

Marjah, Afghanistan, 149, 163

Mavi Marmara, 111, 140-41

Mazar-e Sharif, Afghanistan, 149

Mazen, Abu. *See* Abbas, Mahmoud

McChrystal, Gen Stanley A. (USA): Afghanistan strategy of, 157, 159

McGuinness, Martin: as IRA leader, 62-63, 94

Mecca, Saudi Arabia, 96

Meshaal, Khaled, 36, 109

Mexico: instability in, 184; nonstate actors in, 87

Middle East: Arab Spring in (2011), ix, 1, 9-10; China and, 29, 34, 142, 177; demographics of, 35, 37, 57; de-radicalization programs in, 5-6, 81-85, 179; economic situation in, 35; education in, 35; Egypt's influence in, ix, 8, 111, 114, 133-35; Greece and, 125; Iran's influence in, ix, x, 1, 3, 6-7, 108-11, 113-19, 121-25, 142-43; Israel and, x, 6-8, 10, 37, 121-25, 127-35; oil in, 7; military spending in, 35; non state actors in, 57-100; peace process in, ix, 1, 2-4, 7-8, 10, 15-19, 34, 36-37, 40-45, 48-50, 52, 71-78, 93, 96-97, 111, 114, 121-25, 127-35, 137-38, 141-43; public opinion in, 2, 7-8, 10, 105, 110-11, 127-35; radicalization in, 4-6, 9, 31, 35, 37, 81-85, 167, 179; Russia and, 142; Saudi Arabia's influence in, ix; Turkey and, x, 1, 6-8, 105-11, 114, 121-25, 127, 129, 133

Middle East Institute (MEI): 64th Annual Conference of, ix-xi, 1; W. J. Clinton addresses, 1

MI5, 58, 60

MI6, 61

Mitchell, George J., Jr.: and Middle East

36; and Kashmir, 36, 46; and Lashkar-e-Taiba, 175; military of, 36, 152, 175-76, 183; and Mumbai attack (2008), 175; Musharraf and, 175-76, 178; and Muslim Brotherhood, 42; nuclear security in, 9, 95, 170, 173, 178, 183; police reform in, 178; and Saudi Arabia, 177; supreme court bar of, 178; and Taliban, 46, 94, 167-68, 189; and Tehrik-e-Taliban Pakistan, 177; tribal areas of, 9, 173, 175, 177-78, 185, 188-89; U.S. aid to, 46, 152, 174-77, 185; U.S. and, x, 1-2, 8-9, 35-36, 46, 147-48, 152-55, 165-70, 173-79, 181-89; Zardari and, 176

Palestinian Authority: and Hamas, 42, 74-75; and Hezbollah, 75; and Israel, 124; and Middle East peace process, 124; and Muslim Brotherhood, 42; U.S. funding for, 44, 75. See also Fatah, Palestinians

Palestinian Legislative Council, 93

Palestinians: governance of, 9-10, 42-43, 74-76, 137; and Hezbollah, 75; and Iran, 114; and Israel, ix, 2-4, 15-19, 34, 36-37, 40-45, 49-50, 73, 124, 137; and Middle East peace process, ix, 2-4, 15-19, 34, 36-37, 40-45, 49-50, 52, 72, 74-77, 124, 137; and Turkey, 109; and U.S., 17, 44-45, 74-75; U.S. funding for, 17, 44-45, 75; U.S. trains security forces for, 44. See also Fatah, Hamas, Palestinian Authority

Panetta, Leon E., 95, 153

Partiya Karkerên Kurdistan (PKK): Turkey and, 6, 108

Peace process. See Middle East

Peres, Shimon, 111

Persian Gulf: Iran and, 7, 116; U.S. Fifth Fleet in, 35, 116

Peshawar, Pakistan: shrine attacked in, 177

Petraeus, Gen David H. (USA): in Afghanistan, 149; on counter-insurgency, 58, 168; in Iraq, 90, 92; in Pakistan, 152

Pew Global Attitudes: survey by, 10

Philippines: de-radicalization program in, 81-82, 84

Pillar, Paul R.: on U.S. in Afghanistan and Pakistan, 9, 165-70, 182, 188; mentioned, 150, 181, 183, 186